Spitfire A
Burma and the Pacific

SERIES EDITOR: TONY HOLMES

OSPREY AIRCRAFT OF THE ACES • 87

Spitfire Aces of Burma and the Pacific

Andrew Thomas

OSPREY
PUBLISHING

Front Cover
In response to a series of devastating Japanese air raids on the port of Darwin, in Australia's Northern Territory, from February 1942, a wing of three squadrons of Spitfires was sent out from Britain. When these units eventually arrived in-theatre, they were formed into No 1 Fighter Wing. No 54 Sqn moved to Darwin in late January 1943 and flew its first patrol on 5 February. Although this mission proved uneventful, the unit's gloom was, however, soon lifted.

The following morning, a Mitsubishi Ki-46 'Dinah' of the 70th Independent Chutai, flown by Lts Kurasuki Setaguti and Fumio Morio, took off from its base in Timor on the unit's first recorded reconnaissance sortie to Darwin. Shortly after midday, the duty section of four Spitfires from No 54 Sqn, led by Flt Lt Bob Foster, was scrambled against an incoming radar 'plot'. Soon two of the fighters had been left far behind. Foster was at the controls of Spitfire VC BS181/DL-Y, and his wingman, Flt Sgt 'Pat' Mahoney, flew BR495.

Climbing to the northwest, Foster discovered that his radio transmitter was unserviceable, although he could still hear the instructions being issued to him from ground control. He was told to set up a patrol line over Bathurst Island at 25,000 ft. Once at this height, however, the Spitfire pilots found themselves enveloped in a thin layer of cloud. On being told that the 'bandit' was at 8000 ft, the pair descended to 12,000 ft, and after some manoeuvring they were informed that the intruder was north of them. At 1250 hrs, having followed the vector, they spotted the Ki-46 flying towards them.

At this point the 'Dinah' began climbing to the northwest, with Foster closing from its rear quarter. He noted that the aircraft was painted 'greyish blue', with red roundels on the underside of the wings and on the fuselage sides. Closing astern to a range of 300 yards, and still slightly below the Ki-46, Foster fired two short bursts. Both hit the port engine, but without apparent effect. Then closing to 200 yards, Foster fired once more, again seeing hits on the port engine as well as the fuselage and starboard engine. He followed a further short burst with a longer one, closing to 100 yards and seeing the Mitsubishi's port engine catch fire. Flames quickly spread to the rest of the aircraft, sending it spiralling down until the Ki-46 hit the sea near Bathurst Island. Setaguti and Morio were the first of 18 combat fatalities that the 70th Independent Chutai was to suffer in World War 2.

In his handwritten report, Bob Foster wrote the following brief account of how he achieved the first of his five victories against the Japanese;

'First burst cannon strikes observed on port engine, no apparent effect. Second burst no result. Third burst, strikes on port engine, spreading to fuselage and starboard engine. Fourth burst, similar strikes seen – flames from port engine, which spread to rest of aircraft, which dived and was seen by both "White 1" and "2" to hit the water, burning furiously. No return fire.'

This specially commissioned painting by Mark Postlethwaite shows Bob Foster's Spitfire sitting behind the already burning 'Dinah' as he unleashes his final, fatal, cannonade (*Cover artwork by Mark Postlethwaite*)

First published in Great Britain in 2009 by Osprey Publishing
Midland House, West Way, Botley, Oxford, OX2 0PH
443 Park Avenue South, New York, NY, 10016, USA
E-mail; info@ospreypublishing.com

© 2009 Osprey Publishing Limited

Print ISBN: 978 1 84603 422 0
PDF e-book ISBN: 978 1 84603 896 9

Edited by Tony Holmes
Page design by Tony Truscott
Cover Artwork by Mark Postlethwaite
Aircraft Profiles by Chris Davey
Index by Alan Thatcher
Originated by PDQ Digital Media Solutions, Suffolk UK
Printed in China through Bookbuilders

09 10 11 12 13   10 9 8 7 6 5 4 3 2 1

For a catalogue of all books published by Osprey please contact:
North America
Osprey Direct, C/o Random House Distribution Center, 400 Hahn Road, Westminster, MD 21157
E-mail: uscustomerservice@ospreypublishing.com

ALL OTHER REGIONS
Osprey Direct, The Book Service Ltd, Distribution Centre, Colchester Road, Frating Green, Colchester, Essex, CO7 7DW, UK
E-mail: customerservice@ospreypublishing.com
www.ospreypublishing.com

CONTENTS

CHAPTER ONE
THE CHURCHILL WING 6

CHAPTER TWO
DEFENDING DARWIN 9

CHAPTER THREE
ABOVE THE ARAKAN 27

CHAPTER FOUR
IMPHAL TO RANGOON 41

CHAPTER FIVE
IN THE EAST INDIES 73

CHAPTER SIX
ENDGAME IN BORNEO 84

APPENDICES 88
COLOUR PLATES COMMENTARY 91
BIBLIOGRAPHY 95
INDEX 96

THE CHURCHILL WING

'I had been on standby against another possible Jap raid and was scrambled from our base at Darwin with my No 2. We were ordered out to the northwest over the sea after an unidentified "plot". After what seemed an interminable number of changes in direction, not helped by my aircraft suffering from radio problems, I spotted a lone aircraft and positioned us for a stern attack on what proved to be a "Dinah" "recce job".

'When I opened fire, although I could see my cannon hitting the port engine, it had no apparent effect – and neither did my next burst. Having closed in somewhat, my third burst struck both engines and the fuselage, and soon after I opened up again I saw flames shooting out of one of the engines which spread to the rest of the aircraft. We then watched as it dived away in a smoky arc until it hit the water, still burning furiously.'

This how Flt Lt Bob Foster of No 54 Sqn related to the author the demise of the first Japanese aircraft to fall to a Spitfire. His victim was a Ki-46 of the 10th Sentai's 70th Chutai, flown by Lts Kurasuki Setaguti and Fumio Morio. The aircraft, intercepted whilst undertaking the unit's first reconnaissance mission to Darwin, went down near Bathurst Island. It was described in Foster's combat report as 'being coloured greyish blue with red roundels on the underside of the wings and on the side of the fuselage, with black and white stripe markings on the tailplane'.

This was the first success for No 1 Fighter Wing of the Royal Australian Air Force (RAAF), which had been sent to the Darwin area specifically to counter the damaging Japanese raids following an order issued from British Prime Minister Winston Churchill himself. Fittingly, this organisation was often referred to as the 'Churchill Wing'.

The deployment of a wing of Spitfires halfway round the world had become a matter of faith for the Australian government. A few days after the fall of Singapore, and with the enemy well established in the Dutch East Indies, 188 Japanese aircraft raided the northern Australian town of Darwin on 19 February 1942. It suffered heavy damage, as did the adjacent airfield, while eight

The first pilot to destroy a Japanese aircraft when flying a Spitfire was Flt Lt Bob Foster of No 54 Sqn. He is seen here shortly after the event with Spitfire VC BS181, which he had used to down the Ki-46 on 6 February 1943. The aircraft was named after the girlfriend of its regular pilot, Flg Off John Lenagen (*R W Foster*)

Three Spitfire VCs of No 54 Sqn practise formation flying near Sydney in January 1943 prior to the unit moving north to Darwin, where all three aircraft were to claim victories. Nearest is BS164/K, in which Sqn Ldr E M Gibbs made all of his claims (five and one shared victories and five damaged). Behind it is BR544/A in which Flt Lt R K C Norwood shot down a Zero-sen and Plt Off W H Appleton destroyed an unidentified enemy aircraft – both pilots also claimed two probable and three damaged in it. The third fighter is BR539 in which Lt Flt R W Foster made most of his claims (three destroyed, one probable and two damaged) (*R W Foster*)

ships were sunk in the harbour. Two hours after the first raid came a second attack, this time by 50+ bombers. These were the precursors of some 64 raids on Darwin and the surrounding area over the next 20 months.

With the Japanese sweeping all before them, and with the Dutch East Indies about to fall, the raids raised the spectre of a thrust into northern Australia itself – a fear compounded by a devastating attack on Broome, in Western Australia, in early March. With the Japanese seemingly invincible, and advancing into New Guinea, there was a paucity of air defence units in the region with which to counter these raids. The Australian government thus issued an urgent plea for the RAAF Spitfire squadrons that had been formed in the UK to be returned to defend their homeland.

In spite of aircraft and personnel shortages within Fighter Command, and in the face of some opposition from the RAF, Churchill recognised the importance of honouring this request and duly directed that a wing of Spitfires be sent to Australia with all haste. However, in the event it would be many months before the rhetoric became a reality. Nonetheless, the two RAAF Spitfire squadrons in the UK – No 452 under the command of seven-victory ace Sqn Ldr Raymond Thorold-Smith, and No 457, led by Sqn Ldr Ken James – together with the RAF's experienced No 54 Sqn, under Sqn Ldr Eric Gibbs, were ordered to move to Australia. Accordingly, No 452 Sqn was withdrawn from operations on 23 March 1942 while No 457 ceased active operations on 31 May.

Personnel from all three units began their long voyage to Australia on 21 June, eventually arriving in Melbourne on 13 August, although the aircraft took somewhat longer. They reassembled at Richmond, in New South Wales, in early September and began refresher training. By then, however, the wing's original complement of Spitfires had being commandeered in transit in the Middle East, much to Churchill's irritation!

Sqn Ldr Gibbs arrived in Sydney in late August and then moved on to Richmond, where his squadron had begun assembling on 7 September and commenced refresher flying with borrowed Wirraway trainers the following day. Eventually, the wing's complement of tropicalised Spitfire VCs arrived in early October, and on the 21st of that month pilots were despatched to Laverton, in Victoria, to collect them – bad weather delayed the return of the first six to Richmond until 8 November. These aircraft were followed by

Leader of the 'Churchill Wing' was the RAAF's ranking ace, Wg Cdr Clive Caldwell, who at that stage had at least 20 victories to his name (*RAAF*)

One of No 1 Fighter Wing's Spitfire VCs undergoes maintenance just after its reassembly in Australia. Like many others sent out from the UK, it is still in desert camouflage. Such aircraft were soon painted in more appropriate camouflage, and had unit codes added prior to flying up to Darwin (*R W Foster*)

five more, led in by Flt Lt Bob Foster, on the 10th. Six days later No 54 Sqn performed its first formation flight in Australia, and on 19 November the unit diary recorded, 'The squadron's first "kill" – unfortunately not a Zero, but a stray dog that jumped into the revolving prop of a Spitfire which Flt Lt Mahoney was starting up."

Shortly afterwards the unit suffered its first fatal accident when Sgt Read's aircraft developed a glycol leak and the 23-year-old pilot was killed when he bailed out too low. The following day, No 1 Fighter Wing, which had formed in September under the command of Gp Capt Alan 'Wally' Walters, received a real boost when leading RAAF ace Wg Cdr Clive Caldwell was appointed as its Wing Leader.

By the end of the year the three squadrons were ready for operations, and they began moving north to bases around Darwin in early January 1943. No 54 Sqn's air party left Richmond on 14 January, escorted by a Beaufighter, and arrived in Darwin on the 17th. No 452 Sqn also returned to frontline service on 17 January 1943 when it initially moved to Batchelor, before transferring to Strauss on 1 February. Finally, No 457 Sqn settled into life at its new base at Livingstone.

Climatic conditions in the area – prevailing oppressive humidity, thunderstorms and resulting mud – proved trying for both men and equipment. Wg Cdr Caldwell was amongst those to suffer, for the conditions exacerbated a skin condition and resulted in his growing a beard.

On 20 January the 50th Japanese air raid on Darwin caused little damage, and neither did another the following day. However, the enemy bombers, and their escorts, were not opposed by the Spitfire wing either, for it was not yet operational. No 54 Sqn flew its first interception patrol on the 26th when Flt Lt Norwood (in BR570) took off at 1600 hrs, leading Flt Sgt Varney (BS158) and Sgt Cooper (BR235). Three days later, Caldwell (BS166) flew his first scramble, while in the late afternoon he (BR295) led Flt Lt Bob Foster (BS239) off on an uneventful mission, after which they conducted some practice intercepts.

It was at this time that Gp Capt Walters wrote to HQ North West Area asking about the allocation of unit identity letters, and in the same letter he also requested that he and his Wing Leader be allowed to wear their initials 'AL-W' and 'CR-C', respectively, on their personal aircraft.

The three squadrons were poised, waiting for their first chance of action, which was not long in coming. No 54 Sqn's operational record for 6 February stated;

'A memorable day for the squadron since it marked our first kill in Australia, Flt Lt Foster (BS181) destroying a Japanese "Dinah" light bomber, apparently engaged on a recce, about 35 miles WNW of Cape van Diemen at 1250 hrs.'

The Spitfire had at last been blooded against the Japanese, and before the year was out it would be in action in New Guinea and Burma too.

DEFENDING DARWIN

Tuesday, 2 March 1943 dawned fine over northern Australia, with scattered cloud and fair, if hazy, visibility. At 1030 hrs local time, far to the north on the island of Timor, 21 A6M Zero-sen fighters of the Imperial Japanese Naval Air Force's 202nd Kokutai, led by Lt Cdr Takahide Aioi, took off from Penfui airfield near Kupang. These aircraft would be the fighter escorts for nine G4M 'Betty' bombers of the 753rd Kokutai, led by Lt Koshiro Yokomizo, that were were making the 52nd Japanese raid on northern Australia. They would also become the first Darwin raiders to encounter the Spitfire.

That morning, Wg Cdr Clive Caldwell was on standby with No 54 Sqn, and when the incoming raid was first detected 120 miles away, the unit was scrambled, followed soon afterwards by No 457 Sqn. The 26 Spitfires were ordered to rendezvous over Port Paterson at 26,000 ft. By the time the wing had assembled, the enemy had bombed its target and was heading back north. Eventually, only the section led by Caldwell – who was in his personal aircraft, marked 'CR-C' – made contact, but having been airborne for over an hour he was concerned about the wing's fuel state. Nevertheless, he led the six Spitfires into the enemy fighter formation that was 20 miles off the coast.

Caldwell described his part in the action upon his return to base, initially outlining his attack on what he thought was a B6N 'Kate' but what must have been a Zero-sen;

'I commenced firing at 400 yards and pressed the attack home until I was within 100 yards. One burst only was fired of approximately two to two-and-a-half seconds duration. Strikes were observed on the fore section of the fuselage near the wing roots. At this juncture the enemy aircraft broke formation by making a gentle turn to starboard.

'Being in danger of attack from escorting "Zekes", I disengaged by making a steep climbing turn to port, during which time I lost sight of the enemy aircraft. Shortly afterwards I observed an aircraft strike the water below the position in which the attack had taken place.'

With this victory Caldwell was on his way to becoming the most successful Spitfire pilot against the Japanese. Five minutes later he saw a Zero-sen on the tail of a Spitfire

A bearded Wg Cdr Clive Caldwell in relaxed mode with his pipe, unzipped flying boots and piratical beard, which he grew because the tropical climate caused a skin irritation. He is posing with Spitfire VC BS295 that carried his initials, and in which he had his first successes over the Japanese on 2 March 1943. Caldwell also flew it during two raids in late June when he shot down two Zero-sens and probably destroyed two 'Betty' bombers. Unlike his later aircraft, this machine did not carry his lengthy 'scoreboard'. It did feature a wing commander's pennant, however (*S Mackenzie*)

diving diagonally across his nose. In his narrative Caldwell continued by outlining how he 'immediately dived on this aircraft and attacked from the rear quarter to dead astern, firing approximately a two-second burst. Pieces of fuselage and wing were observed to have been shot away. The enemy aircraft was followed down to about 3000 ft. On pulling away I observed it strike the water'.

Caldwell also noted that he in turn came under attack on several occasions. He found that by pulling as tightly as possible when engaging in turns with a Zero-sen at 160 mph, the enemy fighter did not come dangerously close to achieving a position from which to open fire until the Spitfire's speed had begun to wash off after the second turn. However, by breaking downwards Caldwell easily evaded the enemy fighter.

Also engaged was No 54 Sqn's CO, Sqn Ldr Eric 'Bill' Gibbs. He was leading 'Red' Section, comprised of Flg Off Lenaghan and Plt Off Ashby, when he spotted what he described as three single-engined bombers with a pair of escorting Zero-sens at 17,000 ft. Flying BS164/DL-K, he climbed above the enemy formation and then dived on them;

'I fired a short burst at one of the larger enemy aircraft without observing any result, then pulled up and to port. I felt strikes on my aircraft and tightened my climb, assuming a vertical position, and fired a one-second burst at almost point blank range, observing hits on the cockpit of the enemy aircraft. I then stalled, turned off and followed the enemy aircraft down to 6000 ft, observing him hit the water. When in this dive I noticed that my top engine cowling was pierced and liquid was escaping. Orbiting after seeing the enemy aircraft crash into the sea, I informed base of the damage to my Spitfire but received no reply. At this time I observed another enemy aircraft going down in a vertical dive and saw it hit the water.'

Gibbs then headed back with some other Spitfires and nursed his damaged aircraft home, landing with just five gallons of fuel remaining. He had fired 30 rounds from his cannon and 160 from the machine guns. With a damaged glycol system, Gibbs was lucky to have got back safely. Ashby also claimed a 'Kate' damaged.

In the event, there was considerable overclaiming by both sides, and only two of the Zero-sens were in fact damaged. The explosions seen on the sea were possibly caused by the aircrafts' jettisoned long range tanks. Interestingly, although claims were made against 'Kates', none were present, so they were clearly misidentified Zero-sens. The leader of the G4Ms reported seeing no enemy aircraft whatsoever. The whole engagement had lasted just eight minutes.

The other pilot who made a claim during the 2 March raid was Sqn Ldr Bill Gibbs of No 54 Sqn, who was flying BS164/DL-K – seen here scrambling from Darwin at the time. The future ace made all his claims in this aircraft (*Official via A Price*)

Following this first clash against Japanese raiders Australian Prime Minister John Curtin publicly announced several days later that 'the famous British Spitfire fighters were being used in the Southwest Pacific Area, and that they had already engaged Japanese aeroplanes in combat over Darwin'. Winston Churchill, who took a personal interest in the wing, expressed his satisfaction too, although the glowing terms used by both Premiers made the outfit something of a hostage to fortune.

Ever the consummate professional, Wg Cdr Caldwell recognised a number of procedural and technical deficiencies following this first large-scale encounter with the enemy, and concluded his lengthy report by stating, 'It must be remembered, however, that the Japanese pilots had been airborne for a very long period, and their efficiency must necessarily have been impaired by considerations of fuel conservation and fatigue'.

The next Japanese intrusion came five days later on 7 March when the Ki-46 'Dinah' flown by Lts Yutaka Tonoi and Chokiti Orihara of the 70th Chutai was shot down off Lee Point by Flt Lt Don MacLean of No 457 Sqn (in BR542/XB-Z) and his wingman, Flt Sgt V McDowell. Although this was MacLean's fifth claim, it was his first confirmed. Their rivals in No 54 Sqn noted, 'We had the pleasure of seeing it falling into the sea in flames near Lee Point'.

LOSS OF AN ACE

The next raid came a week later on 15 March when, in good weather with some medium cloud, a formation of around 25 bombers, with an equal number of escorting fighters, attacked Darwin's oil storage facilities and harbour. Both targets, as well as the town itself, were badly hit. The pilots of No 1 Fighter Wing discovered just how difficult an opponent the A6M Zero-sen was during the course of this action, and that height advantage was critical to achieving success against the Mitsubishi fighter.

As the raid approached, No 452 Sqn's CO, Sqn Ldr Raymond 'Throttle' Thorold-Smith, and five others were already airborne returning to Strauss, having been night flying at Darwin. With the experienced Thorold-Smith virtually on the scene, he was ordered to act as Wing Leader, although in less than ideal circumstances, for with other Spitfires scrambled the wing was well spread. On being told the enemy was nearing Darwin, Thorold-Smith and his section began climbing and headed towards the enemy in an attempt to break up the bombers' cohesion.

Several of the section suffered from oxygen problems, and seven-victory ace Thorold-Smith, who was in BS231, was bounced by the escort and came down over Port Charles. It is likely that having landed away the previous night, he too was hamstrung by a lack of oxygen, but nonetheless he had gallantly continued his attack.

Thereafter, in Thorold-Smith's absence no one took over the leadership of the wing, so the subsequent attacks on the Japanese formation

The interception performed by No 1 Fighter Wing on 15 March brutally brought home what dangerous opponents the Japanese were, as four Spitfires were lost. Among the pilots killed was No 452 Sqn's CO, Sqn Ldr Raymond Thorold-Smith, who had seven victories to his name. He was almost certainly shot down by an A6M Zero-sen (*S Mackenzie*)

Thorold-Smith's fatal final sortie was at the controls of BS231/D, which was not thought to have yet been given No 452 Sqn's unit code letters, although it carried his rank pennant. The fighter was lost near Point Charles (*P H T Green collection*)

were fragmented. Although the Spitfire pilots claimed seven aircraft destroyed and seven damaged, three more of them also fell. From No 54 Sqn, Sgt Bert Cooper died bailing out and Sgt Frank Varney crashed, while Flg Off Bill Lloyd of No 452 Sqn bailed out and was rescued.

On a more positive note, however, Flt Lt Philip Watson of No 457 Sqn was commended for remaining in contact with the enemy and accurately reporting their position, as well as destroying a Zero-sen – the first of his four victories. His namesake, and squadronmate, Flt Sgt Rex Watson also shot down a Zero-sen for the first of his six claims, which included 2.5 destroyed.

Thorold-Smith's Section had also included the ex-Malta ace Flg Off 'Tim' Goldsmith, who, having dived down, saw a pair of Zero-sens approaching from the right. One of them passed in front of his Spitfire while the other Japanese fighter tried to get onto his tail. Having claimed 13 kills over Malta in 1942, the 22-year-old was alive to the threat, and he opened up on the aircraft in front of him, forcing it away with smoke pouring from it. By then Goldsmith's Spitfire was also taking hits, so claiming his target as damaged, the ace rolled his fighter onto its back and went into a dive so as to avoid his tormentor.

Having shaken off the Zero-sen, Goldsmith climbed back up and managed to avoid the escorts by diving at high speed after the bombers. Whilst in his dive, he spotted a fighter about 300 yards in front of him, so he gave it a 1.5-second burst that caused it to immediately flip over and spin away until it hit the sea far below. The 13-victory Malta ace had just claimed his first Japanese victim – witnessed by his wingman, Flt Lt Smith 'Teddy' Hall.

Levelling off at 24,000 ft, Goldsmith then made a shallow diving attack on the bombers, opening fire on one of them on the right hand side of the formation. Closing in to 150 yards, despite return fire from his target, he had the satisfaction of seeing his rounds hit the starboard wing and fuselage. Pulling up from his dive, Goldsmith attacked the same bomber from below, raking the underside from wingtip to tail and causing it to drop out of formation. The 'Betty' was seen to glide down into the sea.

Despite the success enjoyed by Nos 452 and 457 Sqns, No 54 Sqn's position as top cover was neutralised after it was bounced from above out of the sun. Leading 'Blue' Section was Flt Lt Bob Foster in BR539/DL-X, who, while heading for the bombers, was attacked from behind by Zero-sens. He recalled;

'I fired a two- to three-second burst at the bombers, then dived to 14,000 ft and climbed into the sun behind them. By then they were heading west. I got above and slightly to starboard behind the formation in line abreast. I caught them up about 50 miles northwest of Darwin when they were at about 20,000 ft, with "Zekes" all around them. I went in on the starboard

The unidentified remains of one of the Spitfires shot down on 15 March is examined, although fortunately in this case the pilot had bailed out. (*No 54 Sqn records*)

bomber and raked the formation to about halfway along the line, closing to 50 yards. Then, as two "Zekes" were approaching from astern, I broke away and dived. I looked up and saw one bomber towards the starboard end of the line break formation and go down to port, with thick smoke coming from its port engine. Another bomber further along the line was also emitting thick smoke from its port engine, but it kept formation.'

Foster was credited with a 'Betty' destroyed and another damaged, while Flt Lt R K C Norwood and Flg Off Granville Mawer each claimed a Zero-sen destroyed. Of their dead CO, Sqn Ldr Thorold-Smith, No 452 Sqn's records said that he 'was an inspiring Commanding Officer who endeared himself to every member. He was a man of enthusiasm and bursts of great energy. He had an acute intellect which enabled him not only to grasp the essentials of fighter aviation, but also subjects as remote as swing music or modern poetry'. In part to mitigate the loss of their popular CO, Wg Cdr Caldwell assumed temporary command of the unit.

After this excitement, the rest of the month remained relatively quiet other than for the occasional enemy reconnaissance flight. During this period Caldwell had his pilots concentrate on training and building experience of operating in northern Australia.

Following six weeks of inactivity by the Japanese, the next big raid came on 2 May. The Spitfire wing's performance on this date would generate a great deal of ill-informed and unjustified criticism, much of which emanated from Australia's US allies. Early that morning an IJNAF formation of 50 aircraft (equally split between 'Betty' bombers and Zero-sen fighters), led by Lt Cdr Suzuki Minoru, headed for Darwin.

Flying BS234 at the head of No 452 Sqn, Wg Cdr Clive Caldwell assembled a force of 33 Spitfires over Hughes strip as the size of the incoming raid became evident. When the enemy was sighted at 1000 hrs, the defenders were in a

Spitfire VC BR539/X was flown up to Darwin by Flt Lt Bob Foster on 1 6 January 1943, where it became his regular mount. He used it to claim one G4M 'Betty' destroyed and another damaged during the raid of 15 March, by which time the fighter wore more appropriate camouflage and No 54 Sqn's 'DL' codes (*R W Foster*)

Flying BS305/DL-J on 15 March, Flg Off Granville Mawer shot down a Zero-sen over Darwin harbour to claim the first of his three victories. He transferred to No 452 Sqn soon after and was killed in a mid-air collision with Flg Off J P Adams (who also perished) during an interception on 26 September (*R W Foster*)

Flying BS186 on 2 May, Flt Lt Teddy Hall damaged one of the escorting Zero-sens over the sea northwest of Darwin and still managed to return to base, albeit short of fuel. He subsequently claimed at least two victories in this aircraft over the next two months. The Spitfire is seen here shortly after its arrival in Darwin, and prior to unit codes having been allocated (*E S Hall*)

The action of 2 May brought considerable ill-informed publicity. One of the pilots involved was ex-Malta ace Flg Off Tim Goldsmith of No 452 Sqn, who shot down a bomber but was then hit and forced to bail out himself (*via B Cull*)

poor position, so Caldwell elected to try for height advantage. By the time this had been achieved at 32,000 ft, the bombing had begun. With No 54 Sqn struggling to keep in position, it was not possible to deliver a coordinated attack. Nevertheless, No 457 Sqn, followed by No 452 Sqn, went for the 'Bettys', with No 54 Sqn engaging the escort.

In a long-running 25-minute engagement, a number of kills were claimed, and many more were assessed damaged, but the action resulted in some 15 Spitfires being lost. Only five were due to enemy action, however, with the rest being caused either by a lack of fuel because of the increased consumption in the lengthy combat or mechanical failure – something that was beginning to plague the wing. Many of the aircraft also suffered from gun problems that were probably due to the weapons freezing at the extreme altitude.

Whatever the reasons, the wing's performance on 2 May was particularly embarrassing following the earlier pronouncements by Prime Minister Curtin. Indeed, the latter was so incensed that he ordered news of the losses to be suppressed. However, a press release issued by the US HQ of Gen Douglas MacArthur stated that the wing had suffered a severe reverse – a particularly galling outcome for all the personnel involved.

Caldwell, however, tried to apply some balance when, in a press interview, he succinctly stated that 'although our losses were heavy, actually in combat we defeated the Japs by two-to-one'. Flying BS234, he had led in No 452 Sqn against the 'Betty' bombers, even though a jammed cannon meant that his aircraft slewed whenever he opened fire. Nevertheless, he was credited with a brace of fighters shot down.

Among those who fell to the Zero-sens was Flg Off Tim Goldsmith in BR526/QY-J – he was possibly shot down by 12-kill ace Lt Sada-o Yamaguchi. Goldsmith had followed Caldwell in when No 452 Sqn had engaged the bombers, and he had managed to down one of them for his penultimate kill prior to the controls of his own fighter being shot away. Taking to his parachute, he came down 30 miles northwest of Darwin.

Going after the escorting fighters, No 54 Sqn claimed two of the Zero-sens destroyed. One fell to Sqn Ldr 'Bill' Gibbs (his second kill), who explained 'the "Zeke" I took apparently had no knowledge of what happened to him, and he turned to starboard and went straight down smoking'. His wingman, Flg Off Wall, said 'I saw incendiary 20 mm strikes behind the cockpit of this "Zeke"'. Gibbs continued;

'The formation broke up and a dogfight took place at 7000 ft. This consisted of the usual figures of eight, each aircraft trying to get on his opponent's tail, but I felt that the Zeros were not very enthusiastic. I saw strikes from my guns and pieces fly off the starboard mainplane of the enemy aircraft, which was then pulling away. I saw seven distinct disturbances in the sea caused by crashing aircraft and one Spitfire spiralling down. I pulled away to port and to the rear, and finding I had only 22 gallons of fuel left I returned to base, landing with just two gallons to spare.'

This was a problem that many of the pilots faced during the mission, and most landed having been airborne for almost two hours – a long time in a Spitfire VC that relied exclusively on internal fuel.

Bob Foster also commented to the author for this volume on the effect Zero-sens had on the tactics employed by No 1 Fighter Wing;

'As far as the Zero was concerned, the Spitfire VC had the

On 2 May Sqn Ldr Bill Gibbs claimed his second victory when he shot down another Zero-sen. No 54 Sqn used beer glasses to indicate victories, as shown beneath the cockpit of Gibbs' personal mount, BS164/DL-K (*Official via A Price*)

advantage of speed and could out-climb and out-dive it. However, as with any other Allied aircraft, it could not match the Japanese fighter for manoeuvrability – one didn't try to "mix it" with the Zero. The escorts were always a menace, which meant that at least one squadron had to be detached to deal with them, leaving fewer to attack the bombers – hence the losses suffered by the latter were not as high as they might have been.'

In spite of all the criticisms made by those less informed following the action of 2 May 1943, the experienced Tim Goldsmith was confident that the tactics that had been used on the day were sound, and after his rescue he concluded his combat report by stating 'the strategical and tactical set-up for the wing immediately prior to the attack, organised by Wg Cdr Caldwell, was, in my opinion, 100 per cent perfect'. Nonetheless, it had been a chastening experience for No 1 Fighter Wing.

Following a raid on the Beaufighter base on Milingimbi Island by seven Ki-21 'Sally' bombers of the Japanese Army Air Force (JAAF) on 9 May, a Spitfire detachment of six aircraft from No 457 Sqn was sent there later that same day. The Japanese returned on the 10th, when a small force of Zero-sens strafed the airfield, only to be greeted by the Spitfires. In the confused dogfight that ensued, two of the IJNAF fighters were shot down by Plt Off Morse and Flt Sgt Rex Watson (the latter pilot also damaged a third Zero-sen). For No 457 Sqn, Flg Off Bruce Little had a narrow escape when BS199/XB-S hit the ground and somersaulted.

Despite the hot reception, enemy raids on the island continued, with the Spitfires having mixed success. This detachment was in action again later in the month when, on the 28th, two sections led by Flt Lt Philip Watson and Flg Off A H Blake were scrambled against a formation of eight 'Betty' bombers and five Zero-sens that were sent to attack Milingimbi. A fight soon erupted with the escort, and although Flg Off Clarke and Flt Sgts Jenkins and White each claimed a

The forlorn sight of No 54 Sqn's BR536/DL-H, christened *Butch II*, after it had been ditched just offshore by Flt Sgt G Spencer when he ran out of fuel during the ill-fated interception of 2 May. On 15 March Flt Sgt Biggs had used BR536 to damage a Zero-sen (*R W Foster*)

Sqn Ldr Bill Gibbs (left) and 11-victory ace Flt Lt John Cock (right) are seen here still wearing their blue uniforms at Darwin shortly after the latter's arrival as a supernumerary in late May 1943 (*R W Foster*)

On 20 June the JAAF mounted a rare raid on Darwin, and No 452 Sqn's Flg Off John Bisley (who had 5.5 victories from his Malta days) enjoyed his only success against the Japanese when he shot down a Ki-49 'Helen', although he identified it as a 'Betty' (*M Goodman*)

bomber destroyed, and Watson claimed one damaged, Flg Offs Blake and Beale were lost.

Jenkins recalled sighting the bombers near Milingimbi, and having avoided the fighters, he answered Watson's call and went after them;

'I dived, attacking the port bomber of the formation from the "seven o'clock" position. Opening fire from 400 yards, I fired a three-second burst of cannon and machine gun fire as I closed to 200 yards. I saw return fire from the rear turrets of several bombers. I broke down to 14,000 ft, as I was not sure whether the "Zekes" were nearby.'

In late May No 54 Sqn received a welcome injection of experience when 11-victory Battle of Britain ace Flt Lt John Cock arrived as a supernumerary prior to being posting to another squadron.

Enemy reconnaissance flights continued throughout this period, as the Japanese were keen to monitor any build up of Allied strategic air power in the area. On 18 June another sortie by the 70th Chutai that escaped the defenders' attentions presaged a further Japanese raid, which came two days later. The morning of Sunday, 20 June was hot and cloudless when an enemy force from the JAAF headed south. It consisted of 21 Ki-21 'Sally' bombers from the 61st Sentai, nine Ki-49 'Helen' bombers and 22 Ki-43 'Oscar' fighter escorts from the 59th Sentai.

Some 46 Spitfires took off to counter the Japanese raiders, and in an attempt to avoid the problems of 2 May, all were fitted with external fuel tanks. Whilst climbing hard to intercept the enemy aircraft, Wg Cdr Caldwell's radio became unserviceable and Flt Lt Philip Watson of No 457 Sqn was ordered to take over leadership of the wing, although there was some confusion about this from the ground.

First to sight the enemy formation over Bathurst Island was No 54 Sqn, which attacked as it turned south for Darwin, shortly followed by No 457 Sqn. The radio-less Caldwell attempted to go after the bombers but was bounced by several Ki-43s, forcing him to take violent evasion action. After further brushes with JAAF fighters, he recalled;

'I climbed above and finally made an attack from out of the sun on a fighter below me. I fired a two-and-a-half-second burst with both guns and cannon from very close range. During the attack both my cannons ceased firing. I then broke upward into sun and observed this fighter descending out of control, and subsequently saw it strike the water.'

Thus, Caldwell described how he had become the first Spitfire pilot to claim five victories over the Japanese, making him an ace in two theatres. He noted, in error, that his opponent had been a Zero-sen, rather than a Ki-43 – a common mistake made by Allied pilots during World War 2.

Also in action was No 452 Sqn's ex-Malta ace Flt Lt John Bisley, who claimed a 'Betty' destroyed, although he had in fact downed a 'Helen' bomber ten miles off Cape Gambier, as he described in his combat report;

'My No 2 and myself attacked the bomber force of 20+ from the starboard beam. I attacked the first starboard bomber from quarter abeam at 300 yards, closing to 50 yards from dead astern. The starboard engine of the bomber was burning when I broke off to evade enemy fighters, whose tracer I observed passing close to my cockpit. As I broke violently away, I saw a bomber burning with both wings snapped off nearly up to the engine. This "Betty" spun into Adam Bay about five miles offshore. My No 2 and I were the last from No 452 Sqn to attack the bombers.'

Bisley pursued the enemy, but lack of oxygen caused him to pass out, and he only recovered when much lower down, whereupon he returned to base to claim his seventh, and final, victim. His CO, Sqn Ldr Ron Mac-Donald, also claimed a 'Betty' destroyed, while Flg Off Granville Mawer in Bisley's formation who had gone after the fighters was credited with one of them destroyed – his fifth claim, which included three destroyed.

Among No 457 Sqn's claims for the day were those of Flg Off John Smithson, flying BS190/ZP-L, who shot down a fighter and also damaged a bomber – he too incorrectly identified the latter as a G4M 'Betty'. Leading No 54 Sqn was Sqn Ldr Gibbs, who recalled 'as I sighted the enemy my engine went into fully fine pitch and I was compelled to drop out, handing over to Flt Lt Foster'. Gibbs landed at Darwin, and he was there when the attacking aircraft came in at low level. In a cool act of courage, he remained in his aircraft and gave his pilots in the sky above him a running commentary of the raid over the radio!

Meanwhile, Foster, who was now leading No 54 Sqn over Shoal Bay, assessed the enemy force as 18 bombers, probably 'Bettys', in green and brown camouflage and in three vics, with at least seven Zero-sens in close escort. He recalled;

'I turned to starboard in a wide sweep to get on the port side and up-sun side of the bombers, which were still heading south. We slowly overhauled them on the port side, being slightly ahead and approximately 4000 ft above them. No top cover had been observed up to this time. I went in on a quarter head-on attack, which developed into a full beam interception. I attacked the leader of the starboard formation of bombers, and held my fire until just 75 yards away, when I gave it an eight-second burst, allowing three rings deflection. I broke down steeply, and on looking up saw one of the starboard aircraft going down in flames. I climbed away to the starboard side of the bombers, who had meanwhile turned east and were heading for Darwin.'

Foster gave chase and had a brief fight with one of the escorting Zero-sens;

'One "Zeke" broke towards me and I gave him two bursts of two and three seconds, one ahead and one underneath, as he turned, seeing my de Wilde ammo striking his port wing on the second burst.'

Leaning on the wing, Flt Lt Bob Foster discusses his 20 June victory over a 'Betty' bomber, which elevated him to acedom, with squadronmate Flg Off Tony Hughes. The latter had made a forced landing during the mission (*R W Foster*)

Thus did the 23-year-old achieve his fifth success, the first two of which had been over the Luftwaffe in the Battle of Britain. Another who claimed a kill was one of Foster's fledglings, Sgt David Wheeler from Nottinghamshire, who, as the son of a rector, was nicknamed 'The Flying Bishop'. He recalled, 'My big day came! I got one bomber, which was a "Betty" confirmed, but my aircraft had plenty of Jap bullets in it, although I managed to return to base. Glad we could outdive the fighters'. In concentrating on his victim Wheeler had overflown another bomber, and almost paid the price when the nose and dorsal gunners each opened up on him.

Also successful at the controls of his personally marked Spitfire BS166/AL-W was Gp Capt Wally Walters, who shot down a Zero-sen for his only victory – somewhat to the annoyance of his superiors, as he was not supposed to fly on operations! Following this engagement Walters drafted the recommendation for the award of the DSO to his deputy, Wg Cdr Clive Caldwell.

Later that morning (20th) nine Ki-48 'Lily' bombers from the 75th Sentai struck Darwin and Winnellie airfields totally unannounced, having flown the entire distance from their Lautem base at 1000 ft so as to remain under the radar cover and attacked unopposed.

In spite of have suffered a handful of losses, the defending Spitfire pilots could claim nine bombers and five fighters shot down, with a further eight bombers and two fighters damaged, in the most successful encounter by the RAAF over Darwin. The headlines in the newspapers on 21 June were thus in marked contrast to those printed a month earlier, and the wing's reputation had been largely restored!

The Spitfie VC's elegant wing planform, cumbersome tropical filter and camouflage are readily apparent as BR537/QY-A of No 452 Sqn banks away in mid-1943. This aircraft was damaged by enemy fire on 20 June whilst being flown by Sgt Harker (*P H T Green collection*)

MORE ACES OVER DARWIN

As June drew to a close, Japanese activity increased, and on the 28th the wing was scrambled once more when the IJNAF returned in force. Nine 'Betty' bombers, escorted by nine Zero-sens, were detected 150 miles to the northwest of Darwin, and Wg Cdr Caldwell led off 42 Spitfires to intercept them. As they closed, he ordered No 452 Sqn to go for the bombers, No 457 Sqn to engage the fighters and No 54 Sqn to make a follow-up attack on the G4Ms. Things did not go quite to plan, however, and No 457 Sqn was the only unit to engage the enemy.

As the Japanese formation approached Winnellie, No 457 Sqn claimed three Zero-sens destroyed and two bombers as probables. One of the pilots to claim a kill was Flt Lt Don MacLean, who shared a Zero-sen with Flg Off Halse, while almost inevitably Wg Cdr Caldwell got in on the action too by claiming a 'Betty' as probably destroyed.

Two days later, the IJNAF attacked the airfield at Fenton, home of the USAAF's 380th BG. A force of 27 'Bettys', escorted by 20 Zero-sens, targeted the base, and 38 Spitfires were scrambled to defend it. The attack plan was for No 54 Sqn to strike from ahead and to the right of the enemy formation while No 452 Sqn engaged the escort and, if possible, also went after the bombers. Finally, No 457 Sqn, led by Caldwell, was to attack the G4Ms from ahead and to the left. After the wing had formed up, the interception took place some 20 miles due west of Batchelor. The defenders were subsequently credited with four bombers and three fighters destroyed, four bombers probably destroyed and six damaged.

As ever leading by example, Caldwell and his section dived on the bombers first, turning to starboard and then making a head-on attack on the 'Betty' at the extreme left of the formation. The wing leader reported;

'I opened fire at about 600 yards, retaining my deflection by depressing my nose steeply. I saw flashes on the port side of the bomber, which I attacked between the wing roots and engine, but it was difficult to distinguish the number and severity of the strikes as most of the return fire was coming from this region.'

Caldwell then broke away, only to be attacked by a Zero-sen, which he evaded. He then climbed up into the sun, at which point he discovered that only his machine guns were working;

'I came up below a "Zeke", which was turning and climbing after a Spitfire. I opened fire at about 250 yards range and the "Zeke" broke upwards to starboard and over, whereupon I pulled over and dived after it, firing a two- to three-second burst from about 300 yards range. I pulled sharply away to starboard as avoiding action in anticipation of being attacked, and then swung to port to observe the actions of this fighter. I continued to dive after it, and at about 5000 ft the fighter began to emit a trail of white smoke, which continued until it struck the ground and burst into flames.'

Also successful was No 452 Sqn's Flt Lt Teddy Hall, who already had a number of claims to his name. He wrote that after having attacked a group of bombers, and with his engine cutting momentarily, 'a "Zeke" attacked me from nearly head-on, firing white tracer at close range. I opened fire and closed to nearly 50 yards with a two-second burst. I observed strikes, and white and black smoke poured from his engine as he flew over me. The "Zeke" rolled onto its back and went down, out of control and smoking. I did not observe him crash but continued to make my attack on the port side rearmost bomber. I gave it a burst. I returned to base without observing further results.'

Hall was, however, credited with destroying the Zero-sen.

The day's laurels belonged to Sqn Ldr 'Bill' Gibbs' No 54 Sqn, which claimed five destroyed, with two and one shared going to Gibbs himself, as he later recounted;

'The attack commenced on the port side of the bombers, and we closed to within 25 yards of the box. Strikes were seen to the port engine of the port aircraft of the starboard formation. Rolling over and pulling out of the sun on the port side of the bombers, I saw a "Zeke" on the tail of a Spitfire and another on his back above me. I closed on the tail of the "Zeke" that was attacking the Spitfire, closing right in almost dead astern and giving it about a two-second burst, during the course of which the cannons jammed. I observed strikes on the wing roots, which emitted thick smoke, and the fighter went into a violent spin.

'I then climbed back into sun and spotted two aircraft falling back out of formation. I followed the bombers in, firing my guns and observing strikes on the port engine nacelle of the bomber in the port centre position of the box. I pulled out again into sun, before attacking once more from dead astern – I experienced no return fire. The port engine was already on fire, so I concentrated on the starboard engine, closing to 50 yards and set this engine on fire also. I made two more attacks on the enemy formation, coming in out of sun and experiencing a certain

A relaxed Flt Lt Teddy Hall of No 452 Sqn prepares for a sortie from Darwin in June 1943. The Australian's final victory tally remains uncertain, but it may have been as many as three and two shared kills (*RAAF via J W Bennett*)

amount of return fire from the centre top fuselage of the bombers, including white tracer.'

At this point Gibbs' oxygen supply ran out, so he broke off his attacks and returned to base, where he was credited with a 'Betty' and a Zero-sen destroyed, as well as a half-share in a second G4M that he shot down with Flg Off Tully from No 457 Sqn. Gibbs was also credited with damaging two more bombers.

Flying BS219/ZP-X on 6 July, Flt Sgt Rex Watson damaged two G4M 'Betty' bombers over the sea near Fenton. These were his penultimate claims (*B Hicks*)

This haul gave the No 54 Sqn CO ace status, making him only the second Spitfire pilot to destroy five aircraft over Australia.

Squadronmate Flt Lt Bob Foster also increased his tally on 30 June when he too attacked the 'Betty' formation;

'I closed to 75-100 yards, firing a six- to seven-second burst, and as I broke away I observed both engines of the extreme port bomber streaming white smoke and the starboard engine of the No 2 bomber of the port vic also emitting smoke. As I broke off this attack, I felt a thud behind the cockpit and my engine began vibrating, with revs and boost fluctuating. I thereupon dived away, and on returning to base discovered that the cause of my engine problems was a severe glycol leak.'

Bob Foster was credited with a 'Betty' destroyed – his fourth Japanese victim – and a second G4M as a probable.

Despite these successes in the air, the Spitfire wing was by now beginning to struggle with aircraft serviceability problems due to the lengthy logistics chain that it relied on for spares and other support – engine maladies were especially prevalent. Bob Foster commented;

'As the months went by, aircraft serviceability became a problem. Although plenty of Spitfires were arriving in Australia, none of them reached Darwin except as replacements for combat losses. For my last action on 6 July No 54 Sqn had just seven serviceable aircraft.'

Even so, June 1943 had been the 'Churchill Wing's' most successful month, and there was a corresponding rise in morale.

MORE ATTACKS

Although it had suffered some significant losses, the 70th Independent Chutai continued to conduct reconnaissance flights with its 'Dinahs' in early July, and these proved to be the harbingers of further air attacks on the Darwin area. The first of these materialised on the 6th when a force of 26 bombers and 21 fighters in three formations targeted Fenton once more. The raid was again detected by radar when some 130 miles away, and the IJNAF aircraft were attacked when both inbound and outbound, resulting in nine aircraft being claimed. On the debit side, however, no fewer than eight Spitfires were lost, several due to engine failure.

No 54 Sqn, led by Sqn Ldr Gibbs in BS164/DL-K, was scrambled and ordered to rendezvous overhead Sattler at 6000 ft, prior to joining the wing and climbing to 32,000 ft. On sighting the enemy bombers, which were noted as being in three large vics, Gibbs ordered Foster's section to attack, followed by the remainder of the unit. In the subsequent fight, No

The wingtip of a downed Zero-sen, still bearing its *hinomaru*, provided an appropriate canvas for No 54 Sqn's scoreboard, which totalled 47 and three shared kills at the time this photograph was taken. These officers are, from left to right, Flt Lt Don Begbie (the squadron padre), Sqn Ldr Bill Gibbs and Flg Offs Tony Brook and Bob Ashby (*B Hicks*)

54 Sqn was credited with four 'Bettys' destroyed, one probable and two damaged. 'Bill' Gibbs described his final air combat claims in his report;

'I closed in and fired from head on, seeing cannon strikes rake the port engine, nose and across the starboard side of the fuselage to the starboard engine – my burst lasted for four seconds. Thick black smoke came from the port engine of the aircraft, which started to drop back out of position.'

Gibbs then broke downwards under defensive fire, before evading a fighter and closing on the bombers once more;

'I now saw only 20 bombers in the formation. I made an attack from the starboard side from beam on the extreme starboard aircraft, taking the starboard engine as my target. Machine guns only were used, the cannons having ceased to fire. I saw strikes on the starboard engine and smoke appeared from it. The bomber pulled violently to starboard and I broke down and then up into the sun. I continued to break away downwards, my oxygen indicator now being on the red mark.'

Once again Gibbs landed with little fuel – just seven gallons – but his persistence was rewarded as he was credited with a 'Betty' destroyed and a second damaged, despite suffering from yet more cannon stoppages.

Flt Lt Bob Foster (in his regular aircraft, BR539/DL-X) also made his final claims during this engagement;

'I took off with No 54 Sqn as leader of "Blue" Section and rendezvoused over Sattler at 6000 ft. We were informed that the enemy formation was approaching the target from a westerly direction, and had been detected at a range of 130 miles. As we neared Anson Bay, we were told that 30+ enemy aircraft were approaching Peron Island from due west, and moments later I sighted the formation crossing over Cape Ford at "one o'clock" to us. We were in battle formation, sections line abreast, at 32,000 ft, while the bombers were at 25,000-26,000 ft and flying in three main formations in vic. I observed no fighters, although they had been reported behind and above the bombers. "Wingco" detailed No 54 Sqn to attack the bomber formation.

'In my first attack I opened fire at the leading aircraft of the starboard formation of 9+ aircraft, allowing just over one ring deflection from 300-400 yards and closing to 50-75 yards, using cannons and machine guns. Strikes were observed on its starboard engine, as well as to the fuselage of the bomber to the right of the one I attacked. As I broke down and away under the bomber formation I noticed the latter aircraft smoking. At the same time I observed another bomber move towards the centre of the formation – it too was smoking from the starboard engine.

'Heavy return fire was experienced from the blisters – it bore a resemblance to large white flashes, and I am of the opinion that it was either 20 mm cannon or 12.7 mm cannon.

'Breaking away to port underneath the bombers, I commenced climbing into sun, and when up a mile above the bomber formation, I observed a lone "Betty" flying northwest at about 18,000-20,000 ft in the opposite direction to the bomber formation. I dived after him and delivered a stern attack, opening up with a one-second burst from 300 yards. This bomber broke down. I eventually saw it crash on land, burning fiercely. As my petrol position was now rather serious, I returned to base.'

Flt Lt Bob Foster was subsequently credited with destroying a G4M 'Betty' and damaging a second one. With these successes he duly became the third Spitfire pilot to claim five victories over Australia – the award of a DFC was announced six weeks later.

Other notable pilots who claimed kills during the raid included Flt Lt 'Teddy' Hall of No 452 Sqn, who destroyed a Zero-sen. This victory may have taken him to 'acedom', as there is some doubt as to his final total. From No 457 Sqn – whose diarist noted that the poor engined performance afflicting many of the unit's Spitfires was becoming increasingly problematic – Flt Lt Philip Watson (flying BR540/ZP-J) destroyed a 'Betty' for his second kill, while his namesake Rex (in BS219/ZP-X) damaged two more. Plt Off McKenzie (who was in Caldwell's BS234/CR-C) and Flt Sgt Batchelor also claimed a bomber apiece. However, on the debit side Plt Off McDowell was killed and Plt Off Lloyd had to bail out. Both men were from No 457 Sqn.

Bombing raids then ceased for some time, in part due to recent losses as well as the fact that the

No 452 Sqn also used a large piece of salvaged Japanese aircraft as the canvas on which to vividly record its 'bag' (*author's collection*)

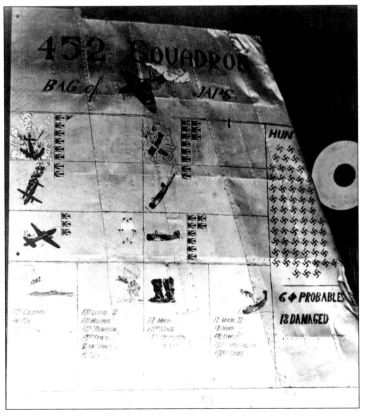

Japanese were now coming under severe pressure elsewhere in the south-west Pacific. However, the regular reconnaissance flights continued, and in the mid morning of 18 July a 70th Chutai Ki-46 flown by unit CO Capt Shunji Sasaki and his observer Lt Akira Eguchi, approached the coast to the north of Coomalie. It was duly shot down by No 457 Sqn's experienced CO, Sqn Ldr Ken James, who wrote;

'Interception made at 26,000 ft after a struggle to jettison my belly tank. I closed in to about 250 yards and fired a two-second burst from line astern. I observed strikes round the port engine. Smoke issued from the port engine and then from the starboard. The aircraft began to lose height. There was no evasive action and he began to spin. When the aircraft was about 5000 ft above the ground it blew up.'

There continued to be occasional scrambles, and serviceability remained fragile. For example, on 5 August Flt Lt John Bisley, flying AR563/QY-R, suffered a glycol leak and had to force land near Darwin, hitting a small anthill in the process.

Shortly afterwards the enemy mounted two small night raids, then on 17 August came a disastrous day for the Japanese reconnaissance force. Three 'Dinahs' of the 70th Chutai fell to the Spitfires of Nos 452 and 457 Sqns, the No 1 Fighter Wing diary noting it as 'a memorable day for the Area'. First over was the Ki-46 flown by Lts Kyuichi Okomoto and Yasuro Yamamoto, which was downed over Chanell Point in Anson Bay, southwest of Darwin, by Flt Lt Philip Watson. He fired a long burst, after which the aircraft's engines began to smoke heavily and then the 'Dinah' blew up, covering Watson's Spitfire (LZ866) in oil – it was the third of his four victories.

Over Melville Island to the north of the town, Flt Sgt Rex Watson (in BS169) made his sixth, and final, claim – including three destroyed – when he shared in the destruction of the 'Dinah' flown by Lts Saburo Shinohara and Hideo Ura with Flt Sgt J R Jenkins (in BS219). Not to be outdone, their CO, Sqn Ldr Ken James, destroyed his second Ki-46 in a month when, at the controls of EF543/ZP-P, he fired three bursts that caused the aircraft flown by Lts Shirichi Matsu-ura and Kiyatoshi Shiraki to crash in flames near Fenton.

Later that same day at around 1630 hrs, the IJNAF's 202nd Kokutai sent over a fourth 'Dinah' flown by Sgts Tomihiko Tanaka and Shinji Kawahara – the naval unit was apparently unaware of the JAAF's losses just hours earlier. Not to be outdone, Wg Cdr Clive Caldwell interrupted his afternoon tea to scramble in his new aircraft, JL394, with Flt Sgt Padula from No 452 Sqn as his wingman. They climbed to 32,000 ft between Darwin and Gunn Point and Caldwell eventually spotted the enemy going very fast at about 26,000 ft.

He caught up with the Ki-46 some 20 miles off the coast and opened fire from 200 yards, closing to 50 yards. In spite of some cannon stoppages, he saw strikes on the port side of the 'Dinah's' fuselage, as well as its tail and starboard engine, which immediately caught fire. He then called on his wingman to finish it off, but in spite of some 'coaching' over the radio, Padula's fire kept missing. Pulling back to 100 yards, Caldwell opened fire again and set the port engine ablaze. His combat report noted;

'The pilot continued to fly on his course, but there were signs of difficulty in maintaining control. I flew behind it for several miles – it was

Flt Sgt Rex Watson of No 457 Sqn made six claims, including 2.5 destroyed, flying in defence of Darwin in 1943 (*via P Listemann*)

Wg Cdr Clive Caldwell became the most successful Spitfire pilot against the Japanese when he shot down the IJNAF 'Dinah' flown by Sgts Tomihiko Tanaka and Shinji Kawahara on 17 August – the fourth such aircraft destroyed by No 1 Fighter Wing that day (*B Hicks*)

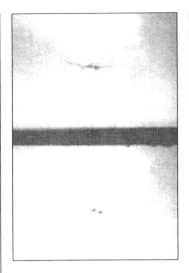

Caldwell's camera gun records the demise of his seventh Japanese victim on 17 August, shortly before he left No 1 Fighter Wing (*via C F Shores*)

No 457 Sqn's Spitfire VC BR538/XB-U is seen here after its undercarriage had failed to lower, resulting in a wheels-up landing at Livingstone on 29 April 1943. Quickly repaired, the fighter was flown by Flg Off R H W Gregory when his unit was involved in the intercept of a heavily escorted Ki-46 on 7 September (*via J W Bennett*)

now burning at three points and trailing white smoke. Height at this juncture was 24,000 ft. Pulling behind, I opened fire again from about 200 yards in a rear quarter attack. This attack was made for practice purposes, and I was certain that it was only a matter of time before it would be completely burnt. From the attack I observed strikes on the starboard wing and fuselage and on the wing root back.

'A fourth attack was made with machine guns only, and I observed tracer entering the port side of the fuselage, following which the enemy aircraft staggered badly, lost 3000 ft and recovered. I pulled out and flew in a position 400 yards to starboard to watch the final results. Shortly afterwards it again began losing height, first gradually and then steeply, until I was obliged to dive at 360 mph in order to retain my position abreast. The enemy aircraft appeared to make an attempt to level out momentarily, and it hit the water at a point 20 miles due west of Cape Fourcroy. I photographed the splash with my camera gun.'

This was the last claim for the leading Australian ace of World War 2, and it also made him the most successful Spitfire pilot against the Japanese.

LAST RAIDS

After the successes against the reconnaissance aircraft, the night raid on 20 August was something of an anti-climax. Despite Wg Cdr Caldwell scrambling with five Spitfires from No 457 Sqn and five from No 54 Sqn, there were no intercepts in the hazy, half-moon conditions. The earlier large scale daylight raids had drawn the comment from Bob Foster that they were 'reminiscent of the Battle of Britain, with one of the three Spitfire units acting as top cover by engaging with Zeros while the other two went for the bombers'. And like the Luftwaffe before them, the Japanese, having endured heavy losses, began mounting night raids.

Reconnaissance missions still had to be flown by day, however, and in light of recent losses, the next one to appear over Darwin – on 7 September – was heavily escorted. At 0925 hrs the wing scrambled after a Ki-46 that boasted an escort of 30 fighters! The Spitfires were jumped in the climb, and in the subsequent fight both No 452 Sqn's CO, Sqn Ldr Ron MacDonald, and Plt Off Tully were shot down, although both survived. The former recorded in his logbook;

'LZ884 – scramble. Oh dear! 1 reconnaissance type plus 15-20 fighters (Zeros, Haps, Oscars, Tonys). Wing jumped. Tully and self shot down and bailed out. Squadron score 1 Tony destroyed, 1 Oscar probably, 2 Oscars and 1 Zero damaged.'

Also lost was WO Hinds of No 54 Sqn, who was flying what is thought to have been the last Spitfire shot down over Australia.

Several victories were recorded by the wing during the mission,

Spitfire VC EF543/ZP-P was the usual mount of Flt Lt Don MacLean of No 457 Sqn. Indeed, he was flying it on 7 September when he shot down an A6M Zero-sen and damaged a second (*S Mackenzie*)

Squadronmate Flg Off John Smithson was also involved in the 7 September mission, using JK225/ZP-L to claim a Zero-sen for his second confirmed victory (*via J W Bennett*)

with No 452 Sqn's Flt Lt Tim Goldsmith (flying JL378/QY-Y) claiming a Ki-61 'Tony' for his final success, taking his tally to an impressive 16.5 kills. Flt Lt Don MacLean of No 457 Sqn downed a Zero-sen and damaged a second, and squadronmate Flg Off John Smithson, was also credited with downing an A6M. Also airborne were Wg Cdr Clive Caldwell, leading 'Green' Section, and Flt Lt John Bisley, although neither pilot was able to increase their scores.

On 27 September Wg Cdr Caldwell was replaced as wing leader of No 1 Fighter Wing by fellow Desert Air Force ace Wg Cdr Peter Jeffrey. Caldwell in turn became the chief instructor at the Spitfire-equipped No 2 Operational Training Unit in Mildura. Amongst his instructor cadre were a number of experienced RAAF fighter pilots from Europe and the desert, including Flt Lt John Waddy, who had achieved 15.5 victories in North Africa – three whilst flying Spitfires with No 92 Sqn.

Also leaving the wing at the end of September was Flt Lt Bob Foster. Posted in to No 452 Sqn at the end of October was very experienced flight commander Flt Lt Ron Cundy, who had claimed seven victories over the desert. He took over from fellow ace Flt Lt John Bisley. At the same time Flt Lt Tim Goldsmith was also posted out for a rest. Newcomer Ron Cundy recalled;

'We were confident that we could hold our own with the Japs. However, the Zero-sen was recognised as being a very capable fighter, with excellent manoeuvrability, so dogfights were to be avoided at all costs. Hit and run tactics from above were the order of the day. Unfortunately – or perhaps fortunately – raids on Darwin ceased as I arrived there.'

Action against reconnaissance flights continued, although these did not always go to plan. For example, on 6 November six Spitfires from No 457 Sqn had an abortive intercept of a 'Dinah' over Drysdale. Leading his section as 'Red 1', Flt Lt D H MacLean (in EE674)

The last Japanese raid on Darwin was conducted by night on 12 November. During the course of the raid, Victorian Flg Off John Smithson exhibited superior flying skill to shoot down two of the attacking 'Bettys'. These victories are thought to have taken his total to four, although the citation for his subsequent DFC credited him with five kills, so his outstanding achievement during this sortie may have elevated him to 'acedom' (*B Hicks*)

attacked the Ki-46 after 'White' section had initially hit the reconnaissance aircraft with several bursts of fire. MacLean then struck the 'Dinah' too, but it still managed to escape by disappearing into cloud. Don MacLean was jointly credited with having damaged the Ki-46, this being his tenth, and final, claim, of which two and one shared were destroyed. The new wing leader was far from impressed, Wg Cdr Peter Jeffrey stating that 'this action reflects considerable discredit on the pilots concerned, and on the general standard of tactics and gunnery training in their squadron'.

On a more positive note, 11 November saw Sqn Ldr 'Bill' Gibbs notified that he had been awarded a well deserved DFC. The following night, the Japanese launched the 64th, and final, air raid on Darwin when nine 'Bettys' mounted an attack. Six aircraft from No 54 Sqn were launched but they had no joy, while No 457 Sqn also put up five, one of which was flown by Flg Off John Smithson, who took off soon after 0300 hrs on the 13th. Assisted by searchlights, in an outstanding piece of flying he shot down two of the bombers. Flying over Darwin harbour, Smithson spotted reflections of aircraft in some bomb bursts and then saw three G4Ms. He recalled;

'I pulled out to port and slightly above the three aeroplanes that I had now passed. Throttling back, I waited until the enemy aeroplanes drew level with me some 200 yards away. My height was still 15,000 ft. I then began an attack on the port aeroplane, opening fire with cannon and machine guns from 20 degrees from line astern, closing to 75 yards. Machine gun and cannon strikes showed on the fuselage, engine nacelle and wings. The bomber's port engine burst into flames and I followed the enemy aeroplane in an ever steepening dive until it disappeared into cloud at approximately 10,000 ft with the port wing enveloped in flame. I did not follow through the cloud, pulling up round and to starboard instead in an attempt to spot the third aeroplane. As this was not visible, and I was not sure of my position, I dived through the cloud layer and returned to Darwin.'

In early 1944 John Smithson was awarded the DFC for his actions that night, the citation crediting him with five destroyed, so this action may well have taken him to 'acedom'. With two Fw 190 damaged claims to his name following a tour in the UK with No 616 Sqn in 1941-42, Smithson had joined No 457 Sqn in March 1943 and destroyed a 'Zeke' and damaged a 'Betty' on 20 June, followed by another 'Zeke' destroyed on 7 September. Although post-war records indicate that he had in fact fallen one short of five kills, Smithson's flying that night was an outstanding achievement. In any event, he had become the first fighter pilot in the North Western Area to shoot down two enemy aircraft at night.

With the change in Japanese priorities in the face of Allied successes elsewhere in the Pacific, the 12 November raid was the last time that the Australian mainland was attacked, although occasional reconnaissance sorties continued. John Smithson's successes meant that in nine months of action No 1 Fighter Wing had been credited with a total of 65 enemy aircraft destroyed for the loss of 15 pilots in combat. Although standby was maintained, the war had now largely moved away. Whilst the Spitfires would see further action, the reality was that by early 1944 there were few Japanese aircraft left in the Southwest Pacific.

ABOVE THE ARAKAN

As it was regarded as the finest fighter then in RAF use, it was inevitable that the Spitfire was often seen as a panacea for most theatres, such was its reputation. This was particularly true in Burma, which had fallen to the Japanese in 1942. The RAF had struggled to protect Allied troops during the JAAF's bombing campaign that had been mounted in support of the Japanese Army. Evacuating all of its assets back into eastern India, the RAF's modest fighter force in the region had managed to hold the line into 1943, despite the units being equipped with obsolescent Hurricane IIs and Mohawk IVs that were largely out-classed by the Ki-43 'Oscars' and A6M Zero-sens that they encountered.

To wrest daylight air superiority off the enemy and to ensure the defence of such strategic locations as the port city of Calcutta, the fielding of even a small number of Spitfire squadrons was seen as essential. Examples of the iconic British fighter had arrived in India as early as September 1942, with the first Spitfire sortie being flown on 10 October. However, these aircraft were unarmed photo-reconnaissance platforms assigned to No 3 Photo-Reconnaissance Unit. A further year would pass before the first Spitfire VC fighters began arriving in India to re-equip some of the Hurricane units. Assisting in the conversion was Wg Cdr Finlay Boyd, an experienced pilot and successful ace.

No 615 Sqn, based near Calcutta at Alipore, was the first to make the switch. Commanded by 5.5-kill ace Sqn Ldr Bob Holland, its first Spitfire

The first Spitfire VC delivered to No 136 Sqn was MA383, which was flown by the CO at Baigachi on 10 October 1943. Upon his return to base he waxed lyrical about its performance! Eventually passed on to No 615 Sqn, MA383 was shot down by a Ki-43 over Imphal on 29 May 1944. Its pilot, Flt Sgt H K Young, was killed in the incident (*via G J Thomas*)

arrived on 30 September 1943. The unit in turn passed its Hurricanes on to Mohawk IV-equipped No 5 Sqn. No 615 Sqn undertook its first sortie on 2 October, when Holland (in JG334) flew a height and pressure test. The squadron duly declared operational, and on 4 October Flt Lt Paul Louis carried out the first Spitfire scramble in India when he launched after a Japanese reconnaissance aircraft that had been detected. He commented after the mission that 'although no interception was made, the performance of the Spitfire was most gratifying in climbing power, manoeuvrability and speed'.

Within a few days the diary for No 136 Sqn, based nearby at Baigachi under the leadership of Sqn Ldr Noel Constantine, recorded 'Today the squadron's first Spitfire VC was flown. At 1210 hrs the CO did circuits and bumps in it for 20 minutes'. Constantine noted after his sortie;

'Lovely machine, light, graceful, fast – oh, so much faster than the beloved "Hurribuses"! Armed with two 20 mm cannon and machine guns, which could be fired separately or all at once. Another difference was that when the Hurricane was put down on the runway, it stayed down. However, the Spit was so aerodynamically smooth that errors in landing tended to be magnified and the little lady would take off again, resulting in several landings per pancake.'

Soon afterwards the unit became non-operational so as to allow it to convert fully, while at Alipore No 607 Sqn also began to receive Spitfires. Having worked up, the two Auxiliary squadrons moved from Alipore to Ramu and Chittagong, respectively. No 615 Sqn flew its first sorties on 3 November when it escorted a Vengeance dive-bomber raid on targets in the Maungdaw area. The Spitfire was at last operational over Burma!

Success for the newly-equipped squadrons was not long in coming, for on 8 November a Ki-46 flown by Lt Ryoma Kimura of the 81st Sentai was shot down in flames over Chittagong by No 615 Sqn. Flg Off Lawrence Weggery, in Spitfire VC MA349/KW-D (which he had named *Verma June*), and Flt Lt Paul Louis, in JL108, had been scrambled with four other Spitfires as 'Red' Section after a 'plot' had been detected by radar. Upon sighting the intruder, the RAF pilots set off in pursuit. Louis' aircraft proved to be the fastest, and he approached first from slightly below.

These three pilots from No 615 Sqn claimed the Spitfire's first victories in the Burma theatre. On 8 November 1943, Flt Lt Paul Louis (centre) and Flg Off Lawrence Weggery (right) shot down a Ki-46, and two days later Sgt Bill Hyde (left) destroyed a second 'Dinah' (*S L E Weggery*)

As the 'Dinah' began to evade and withdraw, Louis attacked from the starboard quarter and set its starboard engine on fire. His second pass caused further damage, and with fuel streaming from its wings as the 'Dinah' began to dive, Weggery closed in to finish the aircraft off. His well-aimed bursts caused the Ki-46's tail and part of its starboard wing to detach, resulting in the aircraft falling away to its destruction. Weggery had got so close to his target that when he landed, his Spitfire was covered with oil from the 'Dinah'. The pair returned to Chittagong at 0850 hrs certain in the knowledge that the

Spitfire had been blooded in Burma.

Another 'Dinah' approached later in the day, but it flew off at high speed when intercepted, while on 10 November Sgt Willie Hyde caught one at 30,000 ft in the same area. Attacking from astern, he sent it down inverted and on fire into the Karnaphuli River. Then, on the 16th, Australian Flg Off Kevin Gannon (in MA338) made it a hat trick of victories for No 615 Sqn when he shot down Lt Tsuchima's Ki-46 from the 81st Sentai – it crashed near Feni. It was not one-way traffic, however, as Lawrence Weggery described when, on 23 November, No 615 Sqn scrambled against an incoming fighter sweep;

The third unit to receive the Spitfire in India was No 607 Sqn. One of its pilots was Australian Flg Off Colin Doudy, who is seen here in the cockpit of LZ975/AF-J at Ramu soon after the unit moved there in late 1943. On 15 January 1944, whilst flying this aircraft near Buthidaung, Doudy shot down a Ki-43 and damaged a second one (*via N Franks*)

'We were scrambled to 26,000 ft, and it turned out that they were all fighters – there were no bombers to be seen. Amongst them was a new model of Japanese fighter. I'd never seen them before, and I managed to latch onto two as they flew away from me. I hesitated while attacking because they had dihedral wings, where previously we had only seen flat winged "Oscars". Anyway, I pulled up abreast of these two and they saw me. One set off on a steep left turn and the other climbed straight up and looped over me to get on my tail. I took a shot at the one turning, but I don't think I hit him.'

Although a Ki-43 had been damaged in the action, the Spitfire of Canadian Plt Off Leonard was lost, although the pilot bailed out unhurt.

There was further action on the 28th when 15 bombers, with a fighter escort, attacked Feni at high level. Among the aircraft scrambled were a dozen of No 615 Sqn's Spitfire VCs, but the raiders were diving for home before an intercept could be affected. Although Sqn Ldr Holland was credited with a Ki-43 damaged for his final claim, the airfield had been hit hard. The raiders returned the next day when 12 Ki-48 'Lily' bombers, escorted by nine 'Oscars' of the 33rd and 50th Sentais, attacked Agartala. Again, No 615 Sqn's Spitfires were among the aircraft scrambled. Plt Off A G 'Nappy' Carroll hit a Ki-43 and claimed it probably destroyed, and he and Weggery also damaged three 'Oscars' between them.

Concerns about a possible Japanese offensive into India through the Arakan Peninsula, in northwest Burma, resulted in the Allies planning a pre-emptive push of their own down the Mayu Peninsula in late November 1943. Unlike the reversals of the previous year, this time there would be no retreat for Allied forces on the ground. If surrounded, they would hold position and be re-supplied from the air.

To provide some reinforcement for the offensive, two experienced Spitfire units in the form of Nos 81 and 152 Sqns were transferred to India (Alipore and Baigachi, respectively) from Italy in December. Once in-theatre, they were issued with the superb Spitfire VIII – soon to be the master of anything in the enemy arsenal. Future seven-kill ace Flg Off Alan Peart of No 81 Sqn recalled;

At Ramu, No 165 Wing was led by the experienced seven-victory ace Wg Cdr Jimmy Elsdon, who had previously commanded No 136 Sqn when it was equipped with Hurricanes (*T A F Elsdon*)

During the raid on Calcutta on 5 December, the only Spitfire pilot to make contact was Flt Lt 'Bojo' Brown, who shot down a Ki-21 to claim his third victory. He was subsequently killed in action on 15 February 1944 (*A G Conway*)

'The Mk VIII Spitfire was a really beautiful machine. It had a retractable tailwheel, clean lines and a pointed tail. The Stromberg carburettor permitted negative "G" without the engine cutting, and it had a two-stage supercharger which gave us considerable additional power flying above 18,000 ft. In the Arakan fighting, we met the enemy in force in our new Mark VIIIs, and within a few days the Japanese suffered severe fighter losses that curtailed their normal aggressiveness. Up until then, enemy aircraft appeared to roam about at will over Allied territory.'

The assault in the Arakan by the 5th and 7th Indian and the 81st West African Divisions began on 30 November, and it was to result in a dramatic upsurge in air fighting. At Ramu, No 165 Wing, led by seven-victory ace Wg Cdr Jimmy Elsdon, with Sqn Ldr Pat Lee as his deputy, controlled Nos 136 and 607 Sqns, while No 615 Sqn belonged to No 166 Wing at Chittagong, which was also led by a Battle of Britain ace in the form of Wg Cdr Finlay Boyd.

Having been fully re-equipped with Spitfire VCs, No 136 Sqn became operational at 'Lyons' strip on 2 December. Three days later the Japanese launched the only joint IJNAF-JAAF air attack of the war in Burma when G4M 'Bettys', with a Zero-sen escort, joined 18 Ki-21 'Sallys', escorted by 70+ Ki-43s. Their target was Calcutta's King George V docks.

Among the first fighters to be scrambled from the Chittagong area were those of No 136 Sqn, while Spitfires from Nos 607 and 615 Sqns got airborne soon afterwards. However, as the enemy formation headed further west out over the sea, bound for Calcutta, only No 136 Sqn and the Hurricanes of No 258 Sqn managed to intercept them. By the time the fighters reached the enemy aircraft they were running critically short of fuel, and only No 136 Sqn's Flt Lt Eric 'Bojo' Brown, ignoring an order to withdraw, pressed on. He claimed a 'Sally' destroyed for his third victory, and his first in the Spitfire;

'I was scrambled as "Drumstick Leader". About 40 minutes later I had R/T trouble, and "White 1" took over the lead. Whilst looking for my No 2, I lost sight of the squadron and proceeded alone on the same course. About ten minutes later I saw approximately 40 bombers, escorted by approximately 15 fighters, at 24,000 ft. There were only two fighters to port of the formation, so I attacked one from up sun that was 2000 ft above me, coming up dead astern of it at about 300 mph. At 250 yards I pressed the gun button, but my guns did not fire. I broke away downwards, skidding and levelling out 5000 ft below.

'I saw the fighters had not followed, so I climbed up sun behind the formation. I then did a gentle dive at full throttle on the port bomber (I think an Army 97) from 1000 ft above. One fighter was diving on my tail as I approached dead astern of the bomber, so I gave it a 5-6 second burst from 400-500 yards, closing to 200 yards. Strikes were seen and small pieces flew off the port engine. Brown smoke and then flames poured from the port engine. I broke down violently into a vertical dive at full throttle and pulled up at 3000 ft.'

In mid-December No 152 Sqn became operational at Baigachi, where it remained in order to cover Calcutta. Soon after dawn on Boxing Day, a pair of its potent new Spitfire VIIIs were scrambled after a high-flying 'Dinah' that was shot down in flames. It was the Mk VIII's first victory in the theatre, as the squadron record book described;

In late 1943 No 152 Sqn was ordered from Italy to India as reinforcement – it was re-equipped with Spitfire VIIIs upon its arrival in-theatre. Among the unit's pilots were several aces, including the CO, Sqn Ldr Bruce Ingram (seated in chair) who had 14 kills. On his left is Flt Lt Norman Jones (6.5 kills) and next to him is Flt Sgt Len Smith (5.5 kills) (*P Huntinford via R J Rooker*)

'Our first Jap bit the dust today! A splendid show by Flg Off R E J Macdonald (JF329) and Flt Sgt R O J Patterson (JF287), one of the high-flying anti-recce sections. Scrambled at 0805 hrs, they intercepted a "Dinah" army recce southeast of base, and after a stiff chase they shot it down in flames. The wreckage was found five miles northwest of Gopalganj. They each got a half confirmed.'

Also scrambled was 5.5-victory ace Flt Sgt Len Smith, while at noon the unit's CO, New Zealander Sqn Ldr Bruce Ingram, who had 14 victories, and Flt Lt Norman Jones, who had 6.5 kills to his name, took off but that had no joy. Two hours later, a raid by 21 Ki-21s, escorted by Ki-43s, attacked Chittagong. Among the fighters scrambled were 12 Spitfires from both Nos 136 and 615 Sqns and 13 from No 607 Sqn.

No 615 Sqn's Flg Off Bill Andrews, in MA290, was one of the pilots to enjoy success during the subsequent engagement. Going after the bombers, his diary entry in the wake of this mission read as follows;

'Had lashings of speed, and we dived right through the bombers. Attacked one, saw strikes on him, very nearly missed ramming him. "Chat" (Flt Sgt Bert Chatfield) also got in an attack, and from that attack two went down. We pulled up and climbed into the sun and then repeated the act. "Chat" got another flamer and mine stayed put, although I saw numerous strikes on him. We got plenty of return fire, and heard a couple of rounds hit my kite.'

Flt Sgt Bert Chatfield was credited with two of the 'Sallys' destroyed while Andrews claimed both a Ki-21 and a Ki-43 destroyed, plus a second 'Oscar' damaged. However, as Andrews continued;

'Through a colossal balls up, "Chat" and I and a section of No 136 Sqn aircraft were the only ones to intercept the enemy. Pilots from the latter unit got three destroyed.

'I was always struck by the beautiful paintwork and turn out of the "Oscars". They looked like beautiful oversized toys, and it was hard to think of them as lethal, but they were, and they could outturn us.'

Of the No 136 Sqn section, Flt Sgt Bob Cross shot down two of the Ki-21s to the west of Chittagong. These were his first kills in the Spitfire

31

and they took him to 'acedom', for he had previously claimed three on Hurricanes in the early months of 1943. His colleague, New Zealander Plt Off Johnny Rudling, had a close shave when his aircraft scraped the tail of his victim, as he described. 'I observed strikes on the enemy's wings and then I realised we were going to collide. I broke sharply away above, but felt my aircraft hit the bomber's rudder'.

Rudling was then shot up by the escort and force-landed at Reindeer strip. Squadronmate Sgt D L Wright had not been so lucky, for he was shot down in flames whilst chasing the enemy formation.

A large raid on Chittagong on Boxing Day resulted in some heavy fighting. Among the successful pilots from No 615 Sqn were Flg Off Bill Andrews (in cockpit), who claimed a Ki-21 and one of the escorting Ki-43s, while Flt Sgt 'Chat' Chatfield (right) destroyed two of the bombers – the latter in spite of only having two hours of operational flying under his belt at that time! (*author's collection*)

ATTACKS UP THE ARAKAN

On the last day of the year came another Japanese attack on the Arakan area when, mid-morning, six Ki-21s from the 12th Sentai, escorted by Ki-43s from the 64th Sentai, attacked some minesweepers off the coast. Spitfires from Nos 136 and 615 Sqns were scrambled, although only the former made contact. Diving on the bombers from 20,000 ft near St Martin's Island, pilots from No 136 Sqn claimed eight 'Sallys' and three 'Oscars' destroyed, with others as probables or damaged. Inevitably, there was a degree of overclaiming, but amongst the successful pilots was Flt Lt Gordon Conway with a brace of bombers and a Ki-43. He too achieved ace status with these kills, having claimed three 'Oscars' in May 1943 while flying the Hurricane. Conway also probably destroyed a second Ki-43, as well as damaging a third fighter and a 'Sally' too. He recalled;

'We had climbed out to sea over the Bay of Bengal, and at something more than 30,000 ft we turned back towards the coast. Looking left, I saw a mass of Japanese aircraft moving from left to right in a southerly direction several thousand feet below me. In the next 30 minutes we put our recent gunnery practice to good use. For me it was one of those days when everything went right. Using maximum combat revs, and a full throttle, I made a series of dive and climb attacks on the fleeing formations, making use of my superior speed from my dives to evade the fighters. As we picked off the bombers, one by one the rest closed formation and dived to evade us.

Flg Off Johnny Rudling demonstrates how he shot down a Ki-21 during the raid on Boxing Day. Seated at right is Flt Sgt Bob Cross, who destroyed two Ki-43s (*Official*)

'From a full throttle dive, I came in at a very high closing speed from above and behind and aimed at the outside bomber on the right. As I opened up with my cannon, the fighters broke around me. To my surprise I saw a burst of fire strike the fuselage, cockpit and inboard wing of the bomber flying ahead of and to the left of my target aircraft. I realised that I was skidding so violently that my shots had gone over the port wing of my target and had hit the bomber next door! So, pulling viciously away and above the defending fighters, I came in in a more controlled dive. Putting my sights on my original bomber, I blew him out of the sky in a tremendous explosion, which was seen by Eric Brown. On one pass, as I was losing height, a fighter climbed up to meet me in a head-on attack and we both fired momentarily as we rushed towards each other.'

No 136 Sqn took the honours when intercepting a Japanese attack on British warships on 31 December, claiming 11 destroyed. Three were credited to Flt Lt Gordon Conway, who thus became an ace (*A G Conway*)

Flt Sgt Bob Cross also increased his score by destroying one of each type, while another bomber fell to Flt Lt 'Bojo' Brown. However, his Spitfire was hit and he had to belly land on a beach in enemy-held territory. Fortunately, he linked up with some Allied troops operating behind Japanese lines and he was returned safely to No 136 Sqn.

Later that same afternoon the enemy mounted a fighter sweep, and both Spitfire squadrons were scrambled once more. On this occasion, however, only one minor skirmish took place. Following the success enjoyed by No 136 Sqn on 31 December 1943, its CO, Sqn Ldr Noel Constantine, received a complimentary telegram from no less a personage than Prime Minister Winston Churchill!

1944 also opened propitiously for the squadron, as it began to receive new Spitfire VIIIs as replacements for its Mk VCs. The first example to arrive was put through its paces by the CO, who performed a battle climb in 'HM-A' on New Year's Day, reaching 40,000 ft in 12½ minutes. Gordon Conway flew an identical mission on 4 January.

That same day, No 155 Sqn finally gave up its obsolete Mohawk IVs and, following a move to Alipore, also began re-equipping with Spitfire VIIIs. Finally, January saw the opening of the Second Battle of the Arakan when IV Corps advanced to capture Maungdaw on the 9th and then moved, via the

No 136 Sqn Spitfire VC 'HM-E' provides the backdrop to a 'team photo' on a muddy forward strip in early 1944. These pilots are, from left to right, Flg Offs D J Barnett and Frank Wilding, Sqn Ldr Noel Constantine and Flt Lts Gordon Conway and Denis Garvan (*A G Conway*)

Ngakyedauk Pass, towards Buthidaung. Further east, the 81st West African Division pushed down the Kaladan Valley, its troops being re-supplied from the air – an activity that attracted the interest of the JAAF.

On 15 January the JAAF returned to the Arakan Peninsula in force, with the 64th Sentai mounting several sweeps over the Maungdaung-Buthidaung area. The first, led by 27-kill ace Lt Gouchi Sumino, was intercepted by 20+ Spitfires of Nos 136 and 607 Sqns. Flt Lt Gordon Conway led the former down on the Ki-43s, which were flying at about 15,000 ft, shortly after 0830 hrs. In the resulting fierce combat, five 'Oscars' were claimed shot down and others damaged. Australian Flt Lt D E W Garvan was credited with two destroyed, taking his tally to three, while Conway, once again flying JL319/HM-B, also claimed a Ki-43 for his seventh, and last, victory, as he described many years later;

'I spotted the first Jap squadron crossing from right to left, slightly below, going south over the beaches. I told 607 we would take this squadron and turned to port, onto the Jap's heading, putting the sections in echelon starboard and the aircraft into line abreast on the wide turn. We came out of the sun behind and above them without them apparently seeing us. I caught the leader with a two-second burst of cannon and machine gun fire from a small angle off with rapidly closing range. Immediately he pulled up violently into a starboard break, with a long plume of white fuel pouring out behind, and the rest broke into us. I had sufficient time to pull hard above those that were coming at me, whilst continuing to watch my man go down until he hit the coast in a large red explosion, which I could see from 25,000 ft.'

However, on the debit side, Garvan was hit and force-landed in a paddy field, while Flg Off D E Fuge was killed. No 607 Sqn also attacked the formation, and its pilots made a number of claims, including one by future ace Plt Off 'Banger' Yates who damaged an 'Oscar'.

Ninety minutes later, a further sweep was made by Ki-43s, and Lt Hokyo, Sgt Maj Takura and Cpl Kondo were all killed as they attempted to strafe Allied troops. Other 'Oscars' were also engaged, and No 607 Sqn's pilots were ultimately credited with six victories. Among the successful pilots was staff officer Sqn Ldr Pat Lee of No 165 Wing, who recalled the first of his six claims (three of which were destroyed);

'On 15 January, when flying with 607, I saw my first Jap. We were above 20,000 ft, and had the advantage of height. The Japs flew in very loose formations, which was sensible. I saw an enemy aircraft being chased by a Spit, and I dived in behind to help if necessary when the pilot gave up the chase. I closed in with high overtaking speed and gave a three-second burst with all guns from astern. The enemy aircraft rolled to starboard and dived vertically into the jungle and exploded.'

Just before lunch on the 15th, a third sweep appeared, and again it was intercepted. This time the Japanese pilots claimed four Spit-

On 16 January 1944, Flg Off Paul Louis was credited with a share in the demise of a Ki-46 whilst flying MH300/KW-S. It seen here three months later after bursting a tyre on take-off at Tulihal on 12 April (*via N Franks*)

34

fires destroyed. The Ki-43s had been engaged by No 136 Sqn, which had been led into action by Sqn Ldr Noel Constantine. He in turn claimed a kill, with four more being credited to other pilots. Despite the inevitable degree of overclaiming on both sides, the 64th had lost five pilots, thus making it one of the Sentai's worse days of the war.

Twenty-four hours later No 615 Sqn got in on the act too when Flg Off Lawrence Weggery, flying his new Spitfire VC *Verna June II*, and Flg Off Paul Louis shared in the destruction of a Ki-46 east of Dohazari. During a five-minute interception they took it in turns to make firing passes at the aircraft until its engines caught fire and it crashed into the jungle. Both pilots had to struggle with weaponry failure during the course of the action, Louis' cannon having frozen, restricting him to his machine guns, while Weggery was reduced to a single cannon, which made it very difficult to accurately aim at the target.

With enemy resistance around Buthidaung stiffening, the last major engagement of the month occurred on 20 January, and No 136 Sqn was again involved. The unit scrambled at 0915 hrs, and climbing to 30,000 ft, its pilots sighted the Japanese over Maungdaw. The Spitfires dived on them, and in a 20-minute fight claimed five aircraft destroyed and ten damaged. The RAF's official history of the campaign, *Wings of the Phoenix*, opined, 'It was thought at the time that the Japanese had introduced the Nakajima Ki-44 "Tojo" to counter the Spitfire Vs, and they employed new tactics, including the use of shiny black decoys'.

Among the successful pilots was Flg Off Denis Garvan, who claimed his fourth, and final, victory, while his CO, Sqn Ldr Noel Constantine also added to his tally. He is believed to have been one of the first Spitfire

Flying his personal Spitfire VC MA292/KW-D, Flg Off Lawrence Weggery helped Flg Off Louis down the Ki-46 credited to No 615 Sqn on 16 January 1944. The large fern leaf below the exhaust stubs denotes that Weggery was a New Zealander (*via G R Pitchfork*)

Weggery's second victory was duly recorded under the cockpit of MA292 by his groundcrew. He also flew this aircraft when he damaged two Ki-43s in a dogfight in late April (*S L E Weggery*)

To extend the Spitfire VC's relatively short range, a cumbersome slipper tank could be fitted to the underside of the fighter, as is evident on this rather unfortunate aircraft from No 615 Sqn. This incident perfectly illustrates the hazards associated with flying a fighter with a narrow-track undercarriage from the rough strips of the Arakan (*J Kemp*)

pilots to meet a 'Tojo' in action, and he later explained that when he first sighted the enemy, he thought that the Ki-44s looked not unlike Spitfires. As Constantine manoeuvred his section into a better position from which to launch an attack, the aircraft were positively identified as 'Tojos'. In his first pass, Constantine destroyed one Ki-44 and probably destroyed or damaged four more. He then recalled ;

'On my eighth attack I was onto a decoy when I was jumped by a couple I had not seen. I went into an inverted spin and blacked out completely. I came to, thought that I was in hospital and called for tea! Then I discovered I was about to crash, put the Spit the right way up and fainted again. I was very near the jungle when I recovered for the second time, and found that two Japs were firing immediately ahead of me. I darted down some gullies and managed to lose them.'

In all, Constantine had been in combat for about 15 minutes.

Tempering these successes for No 136 Sqn was the loss of Flt Sgt Pete Kennedy, who bailed out of his stricken Spitfire and was then strafed by an enemy fighter as he swung helplessly in his parachute.

No 607 Sqn also made a number of claims, including one to Flg Off 'Banger' Yates – he identified his victim as a 'Hamp'. Over the Mayu range, squadronmate, and fellow future ace, Flg Off Wilf Goold recalled the first of his ten Spitfire claims;

'I pulled up sharply at the top of my climb, only to look to my port side and see a brightly coloured Jap fighter – the cowling for his radial engine was painted bright orange. I was on my own, having lost my No 2, and as I could see six other "Oscars" about me, I rolled sharply and vertically down. Flying along at deck level towards home, I suddenly saw two "Oscars" above and in front of me. I overhauled them and gave one a long burst, seeing hits in the cockpit, and he violently evaded. I gave his wingman another long burst, with the same result. I didn't dally but headed quickly north.'

Goold was credited with a probable and a damaged. Sadly, WO G Sole was lost, and once again, in spite of considerable overclaiming by both sides, the day had seen the JAAF suffer yet another heavy defeat. Soon after this action, the efforts of the Spitfire pilots over the Arakan were recognised with the immediate award of a DFC to Flt Lt 'Bojo' Brown and a DFM to Flt Sgt Bob Cross. The announcement of these decorations came at the end of a good month for No 136 Sqn, which had been credited with 13 enemy aircraft destroyed in January 1944. No 607 Sqn was not far behind the unit, claiming ten victories in total.

JAPANESE COUNTERATTACK

During the night of 4/5 February, elements of Lt Gen Hanaya's 55th Division attacked northwards and quickly split the 7th Indian Division. The

Japanese Army again attempted its well-tried tactics of infiltration and encirclement, with its troops carrying only seven days' supplies – captured Allied dumps would provide the rest. The units of Lt Gen Sir Philip Christison's XV Indian Corps formed into defensive positions, including that immortalised as the 'Admin Box', as the enemy's southern force moved on India as part of Operation *Ha-Go*.

This time, Allied troops cut off by the rapid enemy advance stayed in position and awaited re-supplying by air, in spite of Japanese infiltration behind them. The 'Admin Box', for example, received more than 3000 tons of rations, stores and ammunition via air drops. This revolution in supply in the Arakan pioneered techniques that would subsequently be used to telling effect as the Allies returned to the offensive in coming months.

No 136 Sqn (nicknamed 'The Woodpeckers') used the battered fin of a Ki-46 from the 81st Sentai on which to record this impressive tally of aerial victories – 100 destroyed, 76 probables and 74 damaged. These totals reflect the overall successes of all the units controlled by No 165 Wing, with No 136 Sqn's claims being 47 destroyed, 18 probables and 50 damaged (*via C F Shores*)

The launching of *Ha-Go* also resulted in significantly increased air activity. Despite considerable efforts by JAAF fighters to target the vulnerable transports bringing in supplies, the Spitfire units charged with maintaining local air superiority over the drop zones allowed the aircraft to complete their vital missions.

Over the next few days there were several skirmishes, and during the morning of 9 February Flt Sgt Bob Cross claimed his penultimate victory. He had scrambled with three others when, near Taung Bazaar at about 15,000 ft, he spotted 20+ enemy fighters flying along the Mayu Valley;

'We tally-ho'd, turned south and made a diving beam attack. I was to the starboard side of the other three aircraft, so selected two bandits slightly ahead of the fighters that my colleagues were attacking. I felt confident about the attack, having carefully allowed enough deflection when lining up. Just as I was about to open fire, I spotted several bandits behind me beginning to make attacks. I had no alternative but to abandon my own attack and take evasive action.

'Having dived down from a great height, my IAS was approx 320-340 mph, so I swung around and climbed up into sun. I was followed by four bandits that kept up with me until I was forced to flatten out at 18,000 ft and fly level, weaving violently. The bandits started milling about me once again, at which point I went into a spin. Moments later an explosion took place within the fuselage of my aircraft (the IFF set had exploded), and I believed that I had been hit.'

Surrounded, Cross put his Spitfire into a spin to evade the enemy. Having shaken his opponents at last, he then spotted more fighters that he noted had no wing dihedral but had wing armament, as well as a large radial engine with a small wingspan, rounded wing tips and brown-green camouflage. They were probably Ki-44s, although Cross identified them as Zero-sens;

'I picked out a straggler to the east of the main body and made a stern attack, opening fire at 300-400 yards. Thin black smoke soon appeared from both sides of the engine, and the bandit made a moderately steep dive to earth, crashing east of the range of hills. A few minutes later I saw two bandits making for me head-on. One opened fire at a range of at least 800 yards, and I could see flashes appearing from both wings. Our closing speed was fast, but I got in a short burst at about 200 yards and observed strikes on the wings.'

Cross narrowly avoided a collision, whereupon he returned to base having achieved his fifth Spitfire victory.

In response to the Japanese offensive, No 81 Sqn had been ordered down from the Imphal area to Ramu, and the unit saw its first action on the morning of 10 February when Sqn Ldr W M 'Babe' Whitamore led a section of four Spitfires against contacts reported to the east. They intercepted a tight formation of bombers with a loose escort of around 20 fighters, as the unit's operations log recorded;

'Sqn Ldr Whitamore and his No 2 went down to attack, and they chose a pair of fighters slightly astern of the main formation. They got in one good burst, with strikes being observed along the wings of the enemy aircraft. One "Oscar" was claimed as damaged. The Spitfires were hopelessly outnumbered, and after the leader had been jumped by at least six enemy aircraft, our fighters took evasive action and returned to base at ground level.'

That evening, ten aircraft flew a reconnaissance mission over Akyab airfield. Among the pilots involved were future aces Flt Lt Bob Day and Flg Offs Alan Peart and Don Rathwell.

As well as intercepting enemy fighter sweeps, the Spitfire units also escorted the vulnerable transport aircraft as a matter of priority. Five-victory ace Flt Sgt Len Smith of No 152 Sqn was thus engaged on 12 February, for example.

Shortly after 1500 hrs the very next day, a dozen aircraft from No 81 Sqn, led by 'Babe' Whitamore, scrambled from Ramu after 20 enemy aircraft were detected over Buthidaung. Twenty minutes later, at 15,000 ft, the CO's section spotted three enemy formations of 30+ fighters 5000 ft below them. Whitamore ordered Flg Off Alan Peart to intercept them with 'Blue' section, and the latter duly turned into sun and dived, followed by a second section moments later. Soon, all 12 Spitfires were embroiled in a fierce dogfight with the Japanese fighters.

Peart opened fire at 200 yards, but the 'Oscar' evaded violently. His cannons then jammed, so he was forced to use machine guns only when he fired at another Ki-43 from astern and 45 degrees above. Closing to 50 yards, Peart saw his fire hit the engine cowling and pieces fly off, before the 'Oscar' dived away seemingly out of control. He was credited with having damaged it, this being his first claim against the Japanese. Peart then attacked and damaged a second Ki-43 in a tight-turning combat that caused the 'Oscar' to pull up sharply when its pilot lost control.

Whilst all this was going on, Whitamore had closed in on his own Ki-43 from below, firing at it from very close range and causing the fighter to roll several times prior to it diving vertically into the jungle below. It was Whitamore's ninth victory. He was then engaged in another fight, during the course of which Whitamore discovered that he could outmanoeuvre the enemy when in the vertical plane.

Many other Spitfire pilots also tussled with the nimble enemy fighters, and a number of them claimed to have damaged Ki-43s. Flg Off Don Rathwell was one such individual, as he had seen his fire 'ripple' along the wings of an 'Oscar' – he also damaged a second Ki-43. These were the first of five claims that Rathwell would duly make against Japanese fighters.

Upon their return to base, the pilots of No 81 Sqn were credited with one 'Oscar' destroyed and no fewer than nine damaged. Alan Peart described one consequence of the fighting that day;

'This engagement exposed a weakness in our Mk VIIIs, which, at the time, were equipped with pointed long span wingtips. I had to pull up very rapidly with a Jap on my tail, having made an attack that must have overstressed the aeroplane, because following this sortie we found tail rivets that had sprung, the wings had extra dihedral and my radio had been dislodged from its mounting brackets. Other aircraft had suffered similar problems, so the pointed wingtips were replaced with standard elliptical ones and we had no further trouble.'

On 15 February No 81 Sqn was in action once again when, at around 1030 hrs, ten of its Mk VIIIs, along with eleven Mk VCs from No 607 Sqn, were scrambled in the wake of reports that 60+ enemy fighters had been seen approaching Buthidaung. Once in the area, No 81 Sqn's Flt Lt Bob Day spotted the JAAF aircraft, and he ordered Flt Lt I R 'Bats' Krohn down with his section, followed by his own. Attacking from out of the sun, Day opened up on what he thought was a 'Zeke' (it was almost certainly a Ki-43 'Oscar II'), which rolled over with thick grey smoke emanating from its belly, before spinning away and crashing into the jungle – Day had just claimed the first of his 5.5 victories.

No 607 Sqn intercepted the enemy fighters a short while later, and Flt Lt 'Jimmie' James quickly shot down a 'Hamp' (in reality yet another Ki-43).

Faced with such a large number of opponents, both squadrons called for reinforcements and eight Spitfire VCs from No 136 Sqn were scrambled. Sqn Ldr Noel Constantine was successful, and he noted his final victory in his flying logbook;

When delivered to No 81 Sqn in late 1943, the unit's Spitfire VIIIs were fitted with extended high altitude wingtips. However, in the turning medium and low altitude fights prevalent in Burma they caused skin wrinkling and were quickly removed (A H Witteridge)

'Destroyed a "Hamp". Intercepted 60+ fighters Rathudaung. Flt Lt Eric Brown and Flt Sgt J B Dodds missing. WO F E Wilding destroyed one, shot up himself. Very shaky do, and a little dangerous.'

Fellow No 136 Sqn ace Flt Lt Gordon Conway added;

'We had two hard fights on the 13th and 15th, and the second fight left us the poorer for we lost Flt Sgt Dodds, who was found dead in the wreckage, and my splendid friend Eric Brown, whose luck had at last run out. We'd been flying together since our training days at Ternhill in 1941. Jimmy Elsdon confirmed that Eric had been strafed and killed in his cockpit after a force-landing.'

With the situation now deteriorating around Imphal, No 81 Sqn returned to Tulihal. However, the fighting still continued in the Arakan, and on 21 February a raid by a dozen Ki-48s from the 8th Sentai, escorted by almost four times that number of fighters, attacked Sinzeywa. They were intercepted by Spitfires from Nos 136 and 607 Sqns, and Australian Flt Lt Colin Doudy of the latter unit claimed a Ki-43 probable and two more damaged, while his squadronmate, and fellow Aussie, Flg Off Wilf Goold hit another 'Oscar' around the cockpit and last saw it going down shedding pieces from its tail.

Late the following afternoon, a two-Spitfire patrol from No 607 Sqn was passing over Oyster Island when it was directed towards Akyab. Here, the pilots spotted an aircraft taxiing at Dabaing, and as they dived several fighters (identified as 'Zekes', but probably Ki-43s) were also seen in the circuit. Flg Off Jack 'Banger' Yates quickly shot one of the latter down, prior to hastily withdrawing. This victory gave Yates ace status – it was also his last claim. His wingman reported seeing Yates' second burst smash into the fighter, with strikes sparking all around the cockpit and fuselage, before the aircraft disappeared in a cloud of dust.

Two days later No 607 Sqn moved to 'George' Strip, while No 615 Sqn relocated to Nazir so that it could better escort Vengeance dive-bombing raids. The loss of No 81 Sqn was offset with the arrival of No 152 Sqn at Double Moorings, near Chittagong, from Baigachi.

Although there were still some skirmishes to be fought, the action of 21 February was the last engagement on this scale to take place over the Arakan, for the focus of the fighting had now switched further north to Imphal. Japanese forces both on the ground and in the air had suffered serious losses, allowing the Allies to seize the initiative. XV Corps duly began its advance through wickedly difficult terrain, and on 11 March the 7th Indian Division captured Buthidaung, with the 5th Division taking Razabil the following day. The 81st West African Division also took ground as it continued to push down the Kaladan valley.

Whilst the fighting over the Arakan was at its height, another Spitfire unit had appeared in-theatre during February when No 67 Sqn re-equipped at Alipore with Mk VIIIs. Amongst its pilots were several veterans of the early Burma fighting in the shape of Flt Lt Gordon Williams and Plt Off C V 'Ketchil' Bargh. The unit soon became operational. Further afield in Ceylon, No 17 Sqn also began re-equipping with Spitfire VIIIs, causing its diarist to wax lyrical, 'The pilots are naturally all extremely bucked about this, and learning all about them and gazing in awe at these incredible new aircraft'. Both units would see much action in the coming fighting over India and northern Burma.

During the fighting over the Arakan on 22 February 1944, No 607 Sqn's Flg Off Jack 'Banger' Yates shot down a Ki-43 over Akyab to achieve his fifth success, thus becoming an ace. It was also his final victory (*No 607 Sqn Association*)

IMPHAL TO RANGOON

On 17 February 1944, with the situation in the Arakan area stabilised, Sqn Ldr 'Babe' Whitamore's No 81 Sqn returned to Tulihal, near Imphal. Ten days later it moved on to Kangla, on the eastern side of the Imphal valley. Flg Off Alan Peart later recalled 'The valley gave me a strong impression of Shangri-La of "Lost Horizon" fame. It was high up in the mountain range separating India from Burma'.

The unit found itself back in action once again on the morning of 4 March, when a pair of Spitfires was scrambled. At 27,000 ft, Flt Lt 'Bats' Krohn caught a Ki-46 from the 8th Sentai, flown by Capt Shinji Nanba, and shot it down in flames for his third victory.

Also moved north to the Imphal valley was No 136 Sqn, which arrived at Sapam from Rumkha on 4 March and eventually settled in at Wangjing one week later. The latter airfield was typical of the temporary *kutcha* strips in-theatre that were hastily created out of rough earth. These were quickly rendered inoperable in wet weather, forcing squadrons to flee further south to bases that boasted permanent paved runways.

On 5 March Operation *Thursday* commenced, which saw the fly-in of Maj Gen Orde Wingate's Chindits. The glider-borne force landed at two jungle clearings behind Japanese lines that were quickly developed into major airstrips christened 'Broadway' and 'Piccadilly'. Some 10,000 men were subsequently flown in, while the remainder walked! Hiding the operation from enemy reconnaissance aircraft was a clear priority, and on the 6th Australian Flg Off Larry Cronin, who had claimed three victories over Sicily with No 81 Sqn the previous year, shot down another Ki-46. Having scrambled at 0740 hrs, Cronin and his wingman had climbed to 30,000 ft, where they spotted the 'Dinah'. The latter aircraft had previously been virtually immune to Allied interception at such altitudes, but this all changed following the arrival of the Spitfire VIII.

Quickly closing in on the Ki-46, Cronin opened fire on WO Toshikazu Kotani's aircraft. Almost immediately the Australian's cannon jammed, but his machine gun fire hit the 'Dinah's' starboard engine, which soon began to smoke. Further bursts caused pieces of the fuselage to fly off, and eventually the doomed machine fell away in an uncontrolled spin and crashed south of Palel. Cronin thought that he might have hit the pilot, and examination of the

Although poor quality, this rare photograph shows Spitfire VIIIs of No 81 Sqn at either Kangla or Tulihal in early 1944. The nearest aircraft is 'FL-J' (thought to be JF698), which was used by Sqn Ldr 'Babe' Whitamore to damage an 'Oscar' on 10 February and destroy one over the Mayu Peninusla on the 13th. No 81 Sqn moved to Imphal a few days later
(R C B Ashworth)

wreckage later showed this had indeed been the case. The Ki-46 was No 81 Sqn's 99th kill, so a sweepstake then began to see who could bag the 100th – the 'pot' stood at more than 900 Rupees!

The insertion of the Chindit force preceded the next phase of the Japanese assault on India through Imphal and Kohima. Having been thwarted in the Arakan, Lt Gen Mutaguchi had sent Maj Gen Yanagida's 33rd Division from Kalewa, on the Chindwin, against Allied forces defending Tiddim and Palel, while Lt Gen Kotuku Sato's 31st Division advanced on Kohima and seized the road from the railhead at Dimapur that fed men and supplies to the Imphal Plain. Kohima was soon cut off and in desperate straits.

Mutaguchi's objectives were to destroy IV Corps, to overrun the fertile Imphal Plain and to capture a rich haul of essential military supplies. The attack on Imphal duly commenced on 8 March 1944, thus beginning the decisive battle of the Burma campaign. Allied garrisons were soon under siege, and the Chindit stronghold in Assam became the main focus of bombing raids for the JAAF. The enemy displayed their usual qualities – mobility, aggressiveness and endurance – and once again counted on capturing what supplies they needed, rather than having to transport food and munitions from the rear.

The increased aerial activity in Assam had by now become evident to the Japanese, and this in turn led to more frequent engagements between Allied aircraft and marauding JAAF fighters, especially when they tried to intercept vulnerable re-supply transports. As a result, No 81 Sqn was ordered to send a detachment of Spitfires, along with a small servicing party, to 'Broadway' to offer a modicum of immediate air defence for the Chindit's vital landing strip. Flg Off Larry Cronin described the latter as a 'terribly small, and rough, runway. Jungle all round – aircraft drop in from over the treetops. Wrecked gliders lying everywhere'.

The Japanese quickly discovered 'Broadway', and in the early afternoon of 13 March some 40 Ki-43s appeared overhead. In a savage action lasting 45 minutes, No 81 Sqn's detachment destroyed four and damaged several others. Victories went to the CO, Sqn Ldr 'Babe' Whitamore, Canadian Flt Lt Bob Day, Australian Flg Off Larry Cronin and one of the unit's South Africans, Capt Robert 'Moon' Collingwood, whose only victory over Burma took him to 'acedom' (he had claimed four kills in Hurricanes with No 1 Sqn South African Air Force in North Africa in 1941-42). Larry Cronin wrote afterwards of the episode, in which he also became an ace;

'Today, 30+ fighters tried to strafe our new base. Radio Direction Finding very bad – only got five minutes warning. Sgt A Campbell and I were last to scramble. Bounced over 'drome – Campbell killed immediately. I was bounced by eight Japs as soon as I was airborne. Bloody nearly got killed too. Saw them when they were 80 yards dead behind me, firing like mad. Got away from them eventually, and they never hit me once – lousy bastards! Got one destroyed – nearly blew him out of the cockpit. Makes my score five destroyed. In all we got four and lost one.'

Appropriately, it was the CO's kill that took No 81 Sqn to its century, and he claimed the cash prize! The action was witnessed by the Air Officer Commanding, AVM Stanley Vincent, who was himself a World War 1 ace. He was delighted to see the Spitfires outperforming the Ki-43s.

On the morning of 6 March 1944 Flg Off Larry Cronin of No 81 Sqn shot down a Ki-46 near Imphal. This was his fourth victory, and it was recorded in the unit's 'Ace of Spades' marking on the nose of his Spitfire VIII. The 'Dinah' was No 81 Sqn's 99th victory of the war (*via C F Shores*)

Aside from the loss of Campbell, several of the No 81 Sqn Spitfires had also been damaged in this fierce fight, so the surviving aircraft were returned to Tulihal to be repaired. Over the next few days further patrols were flown from 'Broadway', although the JAAF remained conspicuous by its absence until the 16th. Shortly after a dawn raid on the airstrip, six Spitfires were scrambled from 'Broadway' and a series of dogfights took place over Paungbyin. Peart, who had flown in to the airstrip soon after dawn, destroyed a Ki-43 'Oscar'. Flying 'FL-B', he wrote in his logbook of his elevation to 'acedom', 'Scramble. Intercepted two gaggles of Zeros and Oscars. Wizard scrap. One Zero damaged and one Oscar destroyed'.

At Imphal that same morning No 136 Sqn was also scrambled soon after 0800 hrs when nine Spitfires, led by Flg Off Vern Butler, were sent after 30+ 'Oscar IIs' that had been detected over the Kabaw Valley at between 20,000-30,000 ft. The RAF pilots got above the enemy fighters and then dived on them, with Flt Sgt Bob Cross getting off a long burst at a straggler, thought to have been flown by 1Lt Toshio Ohtsubo of the 204th Sentai – the 'Oscar' crashed near Palel. Cross' sixth Spitfire victory was his ninth overall, and it made him the most successful RAF pilot against the Japanese. Bob Cross was described by a colleague thus;

'He was very much a reclusive, almost withdrawn, chap who, whilst not unsociable, tended to keep very much to himself. But he would frequently drop what he was doing, pick up his kit and walk out to his aircraft, telling his crew the squadron would be scrambled in x-number of minutes – and it was! He was a quiet, unassuming chap, with eyes like a hawk for spotting Jap aircraft at great distances in the vastness of the sky.'

No 81 Sqn's last, and most traumatic, day at 'Broadway' started as normal when the CO, Sqn Ldr Whitamore, led the detachment in at dawn on the 17th. Once the warning of incoming 'hostiles' had been given, he and Flg Off Peart scrambled, leaving the others in reserve. As the pair struggled off the marshy surface, a quartet of 'Oscars' appeared overhead and began their strafing attack. Alan Peart vividly recalled;

'I remember Whitamore hauling his machine off the ground with emergency boost. I did the same. We had to do a crazy manoeuvre – a kind of stall turn off the ground – to try and get behind the Ki-43s to stop their strafing run. I don't think that we were very successful.'

As the two Spitfires tried to escape, a much larger formation of Ki-43s appeared, and Whitamore was soon fighting for his life, shooting one down before he succumbed. Alan Peart saw him fall, and then fought a desperate 40-minute battle for his own survival;

'The dogfight, which seldom reached above 2000 ft, tested both me and my machine, and was confined to an area of about five miles' radius. Two "Oscars" were shot down for the loss of one Spitfire, but our other fighters had been shot-up on the ground. By the end of the scrap I was so exhausted that I was just looking for a place to crash-land, rather than let myself be shot down – there was nowhere else I could go. I could hardly move I was so exhausted. Suddenly, there weren't any Jap fighters – they'd gone.'

Peart had managed to shoot down one of the Ki-43s, and he subsequently received a DFC for his gallantry. In his flying logbook he wrote of his sortie, 'Scramble. Zeros strafed airfield. CO shot down. Plt Off W J Coulter killed. Very nearly bought it in scrap. One Oscar

On 16 March 1944, Flt Sgt Bob Cross of No 136 Sqn shot down a Ki-43 over the Kabaw Valley. This was his sixth, and final, Spitfire victory. With three previous kills on Hurricanes, his tally of nine victories made him the most successful RAF fighter pilot in Burma (*via C F Shores*)

Flg Off Alan Peart of No 81 Sqn was lucky to survive the traumas of the 'Broadway' detachment on 17 March, having 'made ace' the previous day (*A Peart via N Franks*)

43

destroyed. Confirmed by Army'. Having been caught on the ground, the other aircraft were damaged. Capt A D Maclean and Casson had remarkable escapes, as they were sat in their cockpits when hit, but Flg Off Coulter died from his wounds. The survivors were flown out that night.

Whitamore's loss was a severe blow to the squadron, which, after its recent traumas, flew some uneventful scrambles for the rest of the day. On 19 March No 615 Sqn moved to Silchar West to reinforce the Imphal area, although it was not based in the valley itself, while No 155 Sqn and its new Spitfire VIIIs joined No 293 Wing (which was now led by 21-victory ace Wg Cdr R F Boyd) near Calcutta.

UNDER SIEGE

A few days later, the effectiveness of the defending fighters at Imphal was further reduced when the radar site at Tamu, on the Burma-India border, fell as the army fell back onto Imphal. The situation for the Allies worsened on 28 March when Japanese forces cut the road to Dimapur, thus completing the encirclement of the Imphal valley and the siege of its garrison. The latter would now have to rely exclusively on air support units for its survival.

No 81 Sqn eventually withdrew to Kumbhirgram, but it retained detachments at Tulihal, Kangla and Palel. Aircraft would be flown to these strips each morning, and from here pilots would maintain patrols over the Chindits' lifeline at 'Broadway'.

Soon after dawn on 28 March, No 81 Sqn scrambled ten Spitfires from Tulihal to intercept a group of Ki-43s that had been strafing in the Tamu area. Using their height advantage over the JAAF fighters, Flt Lt Bob Day quickly shot one of the fighters down to claim his third victory and Flt Lt 'Bats' Krohn was credited with a probable and two damaged. The following day the unit welcomed its new CO, Sqn Ldr J V Marshall.

Further south from Ramu near Cox's Bazaar, in Bengal, No 152 Sqn began long range operations on 30 March when it escorted USAAF P-38 Lightnings in an attack on Meiktila, in central Burma. However, when near Rainghat, in the rugged Arakan hills, during the return leg of a sweep on 1 April, 6.5-kill ace Flt Lt Norman Jones found that he could not switch to his overload tank and he was forced to bail out of JF666. Landing safely in the jungle, he was fortunate to be picked up by an army patrol. Flt Sgt Berry had no such luck when he suffered a similar problem several days later – no trace of him was ever found.

During the first two weeks of April the JAAF made great efforts to break Imphal's vital air supply route, with two Dakotas from No 194 Sqn being shot down on the 7th and 9th in spite of the best efforts of the escorting Spitfires. On 11 April, for example, No 136 Sqn tangled inconclusively with marauding 'Oscars', whilst the following afternoon some 30 Ki-43s of the 64th Sentai undertook a sweep over

One of No 81 Sqn's aircraft wears the leaping panther of No 152 Sqn in a light hearted gesture during the fighting at Imphal (*N Franklin*)

Imphal. They clashed with Spitfires over Homalin, and one of the latter was claimed to have been destroyed by nine-kill ace Maj Yoshio Hirose. The 'Oscar' pilots had been engaged by ten Spitfires from No 81 Sqn, and two Ki-43s were damaged – one of these was credited to Flg Off Larry Cronin as his final combat claim. The following day No 607 Sqn flew up to Wangjing to replace No 136 Sqn, which then withdrew to Chittagong. There, it replaced No 152 Sqn, which had moved down the coast to Rumkha, at the top of the Mayu Peninsula.

Throughout this period the JAAF further increased its aerial activity in an effort to support the advance of its troops. Spitfire units in turn found themselves engaging formations of Ki-43s on a near daily basis. During the late afternoon of 13 April, 'Oscars' from the 50th and 64th Sentais escorted nine Ki-48s from the 8th Sentai that had been sent to attack Allied troops in Mawlu. The defending fighter units failed to claim any successes against this well organised raid, but a repeat attack on Imphal on the morning of the 15th did not go so well for the JAAF.

Twenty-two Spitfires from Nos 81 and 136 Sqns were scrambled to intercept the raiders, and as the RAF fighters climbed to the south, the 50-strong JAAF formation was spotted. Having gained a height advantage, No 81 Sqn dived on 12 Ki-43s, one of which was shot down by future ace Flg Off Don Rathwell, who also claimed another one damaged. Trailing the raid towards Imphal, No 136 Sqn also eventually attacked, but it was driven off by the escorts. Despite the best efforts of the Spitfire pilots, the raid caused considerable damage.

As the fighting on the ground intensified, so the JAAF's aerial offensive was also stepped up a gear, with daily sweeps over the Imphal area by large formations of fighters and bombers. On the afternoon of 17 April 50+ Ki-43s drawn from the 50th, 64th and 204th Sentais covered just six Ki-21 'Sallys' in an attack on Imphal. 'Oscars' from the 50th Sentai initially flew a sweep ahead of the main formation, which was heading for Palel. However, before the latter could reach their target they were engaged by high-flying Spitfires from Nos 81 and 607 Sqns that then followed the enemy towards Tamu. Flg Off Alan Peart, in JG349/FL-D, recalled scoring his final kill during this mission;

'We were scrambled from the strip on a clear day, and I think I was leading B Flight's four Spitfires. We climbed hard under instruction from the controller and intercepted a large enemy force. There were six bombers at 15,000 ft, with covering fighters up to 30,000 ft. We positioned ourselves and then attacked the top cover. At high altitude the Japanese aircraft performed poorly in comparison with the Spitfire, and they rapidly joined their medium cover fighters. This is where the main combat took place.

'The "Oscar" I claimed destroyed was badly hit, and it fell out of the sky out of control. The fighter spun, recovered, spun and recovered in that sequence until a gout of flame appeared from the jungle below me. I was assembling my flight for a further attack when a second "Oscar" came up from underneath me, firing in my direction until he could climb no more – he then stall-turned away. As we were assembling I only took evasive action, and did not press home this further good opportunity.

'The Spitfire VIII had a considerable advantage over the "Oscar II" during engagements such as this one, for it had better armoured protection, more firepower, was faster and, because of its two-stage supercharger, enjoyed superior performance at altitude. The Ki-43-II, on the other hand, was extremely manoeuvrable, had greater endurance and generally outnumbered the intercepting Spitfires.

'Our tactics were to position ourselves above the "Oscars" and attack at speed out of the sun, therefore surprising them if possible. We would then apply plenty of power to climb away out of range. Thus, we could mount continuous attacks with relative impunity.'

Alan Peart also claimed two 'Oscars' damaged during this clash, while his SAAF colleague, Lt J G White, was credited with a Ki-43 probably destroyed and a Ki-21 damaged.

The JAAF kept the pressure up on the Spitfire units when, on 21 April, 28 'Oscars' strafed targets in the Imphal area, with Kangla being the main focus of their attention. The next day 20 more attacked Tulihal. On the 24th, while returning from a rare uneventful patrol, Flt Lt Bob Day and his wingman were vectored onto a Ki-46 of the 81st Sentai, flown by Capt Taisuke Honma. The 'Dinah' literally fell apart under the combined fire of the two Spitfires, and the half share that Day received following its demise proved to be the 27-year-old Canadian's final victory with No 81 Sqn. He would subsequently achieve ace status on 9 January 1945 while commanding Spitfire VIII-equipped No 67 Sqn.

No 81 Sqn was in action once again on 25 April, when, shortly before 0730 hrs, eight Spitfires were scrambled against an incoming raid of around 30 fighters. In the resulting fight, Flt Lt 'Bats' Krohn (in JG348) damaged three 'Oscars', although his fighter was also hit. Other pilots claimed two more damaged and a probable, while Don Rathwell, who was flying JG333, destroyed one to claim his fifth victim, and so join the elite company of aces. Yet despite these best efforts the JAAF still managed to intercept the vulnerable Dakotas and shoot three of them down.

Later that same morning No 615 Sqn was ordered off, and amongst those pilots scrambled to intercept 'Oscars' spotted 40 miles from Silchar was Australian pilot Flt Lt Kevin Gannon. He subsequently reported;

'Dived down from 11,000 ft to 5000 ft and attacked the rear enemy aircraft of the main four, which were by this time turning to port. Gave one long burst of cannon and machine gun fire, closing in from 450 to 60 yards. The "Oscar" pulled up sharply, went over almost on its back and dived away to port with clouds of white smoke pouring from its engine.'

Gannon was unable to see if his target had hit the ground, for he was set upon by several other Ki-43s and forced to perform some violent evasive manoeuvring in order to escape. He duly claimed a probable.

Japanese fighters were again active over the Imphal valley on 26 April when they escorted Ki-48s to their targets. As they headed north, the formation encountered a lone USAAF B-29 that the 'Oscar' pilots made short work of – it was one of the first examples of the Superfortress to be shot down in this area.

After this distraction, the formation approached Imphal, where Spitfires from both Auxiliary units (Nos 607 and 615) and No 81 Sqn were scrambled. They were still in the climb, however, when Tulihal was hit. No 607 Sqn was then ordered back to Sapam, where a number of Japanese aircraft were engaged. Flt Lt Coombes damaged two 'Oscars' and his wingman, Flg Off Horace Taylor (who held an MBE), claimed another as a probable. No 615 Sqn also got into the action at this point, and its Australian CO, Sqn Ldr D W McCormack, claimed a probable, as did Flg Off Andrew, while Flg Off 'Nappy' Carroll was credited with one damaged – his fifth, and final, claim. Flying in his personally marked aircraft, Flt Lt Sydney Weggery also made his final claims, as he later described;

'Attacked one "Oscar" from the starboard rear quarter, firing a short burst of cannon and machine gun and closing in from 150 to 50 yards. Several strikes were seen along the starboard wing. Enemy aircraft turned sharply to starboard, losing height, and own aircraft pulled up, so I lost sight of it. Damaged.'

Two days later yet another Ki-46 was lost when Capt Kazuya Ohata's aircraft failed to return. He had fallen victim to No 607 Sqn's Plt Off G A N Curnock and Flt Sgt Townend.

On 29 April Spitfires from Nos 136 and 152 Sqns (the latter based in Bengal) mounted a strafing raid on Meiktila and Kangaung. In a brief combat with Ki-43s over Kangaung, Flg Off Johnny Rudling was shot down in flames and killed whilst going to the aid of a colleague – a tragic end to a selfless act by the experienced New Zealander, who had served with No 136 Sqn since July 1942.

The units up in Assam were also looking to increase the range of their Spitfires so as to conduct longer range offensive sweeps, in spite of the increasing rain and indifferent weather. Capt 'Moon' Collingwood, Don Rathwell, Bob Day and others duly collected external tanks in late April.

On May Day, whilst in the final stages of preparing for a move up to Comilla, a pair of No 152 Sqn Spitfire VIIIs were scrambled and they shot down a 'Dinah' (flown by Maj Akira Anzai) off Oyster Island. Once settled into its new base, No 152 Sqn regularly flew patrols into the Imphal valley so as to provide some relief for No 81 Sqn.

2 May saw Wg Cdr Pat Lee – recalled by a contemporary as 'a bit of a roving wing leader, and a hell of a nice guy' – assume command of No 170 Wing, which included Nos 81 and 136 Sqns. He replaced Wg Cdr Henry Goddard.

May 1944 was probably the busiest month for air combat throughout the entire Burma campaign, despite the deteriorating weather. The JAAF continued to support the ground fighting around Imphal and Kohima, and early on the 6th, 12 Spitfires from No 607 Sqn were scrambled against a raid consisting of 20 Ki-43s from the 50th Sentai. Two Japanese fighters were claimed destroyed by Flt Lt L G Coons and Plt Off D L Stuart. Forty-eight hours later the squadron escorted a daylight bombing raid on Japanese positions.

On 10 May No 615 Sqn moved to Dergaon so as to take over the role of patrolling the vital Assam valley air transport corridor from No 81 Sqn. Early the next morning No 607 Sqn was in action again when it engaged Ki-43s from the veteran 64th Sentai that were attacking Palel. Diving unseen on the fighters, Flg Off Wilf Goold (in LV755/AF-Z) set one on fire and saw Cpl Heiji Shinohara bail out – this was the Australian's fourth victory. A second 'Oscar' was claimed by Flt Sgt H Saunby.

Kohima endured a further attack by 24+ Ki-43s at 0715 hrs, and some of these were bounced near Palel by more Spitfires from No 607 Sqn. Flt Lt Mike Coombes, in company with Flt Sgt J P Haley, attacked fighters

A Ki-43 is caught on the camera gun film exposed by No 607 Sqn's CO, Sqn Ldr G G A Davies, on 10 May. He claimed it damaged (*via N Franks*)

from the 50th Sentai that were decorated with distinctive yellow fuselage flashes. Both hit Ki-43s with their fire, Coombes catching one from dead astern. He reported that his rounds caused the cockpit to explode, before the 'Oscar' rolled slowly to the left and dived into the ground semi-inverted. This was probably the fighter flown by Sgt Maj Koichi Nagumo, who was on his first operational sortie.

Three hours later, at around 1015 hrs, Flg Off Goold led a section off after enemy fighters were detected northeast of Imphal. Once in the area, he spotted several 'Oscars', and Flt Lt J L Briggs' section went after them. Flg Off C E M B Hole was credited with a victory, while Burmese pilot Flg Off S S 'Sammy' Shi Sho claimed another one damaged. Flying top cover above his section mates, Plt Off D Caldwell (in JG201/AF-C) spotted yet another 'Oscar' immediately below him. Diving down onto its tail, he saw his rounds strike just aft of the cockpit and pieces break off as it dived into a hillside.

No 81 Sqn was also scrambled to engage these aircraft, and Flg Off Alan Peart was credited with one damaged as his final claim.

By mid-May Allied forces had begun to retake lost ground from the Japanese, although the struggle at Imphal continued unabated, resulting in further heavy air fighting. During the morning of the 18th, a bombing raid on Imphal was intercepted by aircraft from both Nos 81 and 607 Sqns, the Spitfire pilots having clawed their way up to 26,000 ft in order to engage the bombers. JAAF aircraft had initially been detected some 50 miles southwest of Palel, resulting in four No 81 Sqn machines being scrambled. The rest of the unit had taken off a short while later.

Flg Off E J Filshie's section made contact first, and he claimed an 'Oscar' as a probable. It was then No 607 Sqn's turn to engage the enemy, the unit being led by Flg Off Wilf Goold, as his CO's radio was unserviceable. Goold went for two Ki-43s flying in line astern, but his targets successfully evaded. Pulling up, he then got in behind another 'Oscar' and shot up its tail before the enemy pilot also wildly evaded. Goold then went for a third fighter that he succeeded in hitting from 300 yards as it banked sharply to the left. This machine went down trailing flames from its cowling, and the fighter was seen to crash south of Bishenpur. Goold had just scored his fifth kill.

Other pilots from both units made further claims totalling six probables and nine damaged, although No 81 Sqn lost Flg Off D H Hamblyn in return – his Spitfire was shot up by a Ki-43 and he crash-landed near Moirang.

May's heavy fighting continued one week later on the 25th when four of No 607 Sqn's Spitfires that were on an early patrol in the transport corridor to the south of Sapam spotted five Ki-43s, with others above them as top cover. Unit CO Sqn Ldr Davies led the section (text continues on page 58)

Whilst defending Palel on 18 May, No 607 Sqn's Flg Off Wilf Goold shot down a Ki-43 and damaged two more. These were his final claims, and they took him to 'acedom' (*No 607 Sqn Association*)

48

1
Spitfire VC BS295/CR-C of Wg Cdr C R Caldwell, No 1 Fighter Wing, Strauss, Northern Territory, March 1943

2
Spitfire VC BS231/D of Sqn Ldr R E Thorold-Smith, No 452 Sqn RAAF, Strauss, Northern Territory, March 1943

3
Spitfire VC BR539/DL-X of Flt Lt R W Foster, No 54 Sqn, Winnellie, Northern Territory, March-July 1943

4
Spitfire VC BS186/QY-L of Flt Lt E S Hall, No 452 Sqn RAAF, Strauss, Northern Territory, March-June 1943

5
Spitfire VC BS164/DL-K of Sqn Ldr E M Gibbs, No 54 Sqn, Winnellie, Northern Territory, May 1943

6
Spitfire VC BS305/DL-J of Flt Lt J R Cock, No 54 Sqn, Winnellie, Northern Territory, 1 June 1943

7
Spitfire VC JG740/UP-U of Sqn Ldr A C Rawlinson, No 79 Sqn RAAF, Vivigangi and Kiriwina, New Guinea, June-November 1943

8
Spitfire VC JK225/ZP-L of Flg Off J H Smithson, No 452 Sqn RAAF, Strauss, Northern Territory, September 1943

9
Spitfire VC LZ862 of Flt Lt J L Waddy, No 2 OTU, Mildura, Victoria, September 1943-February 1944

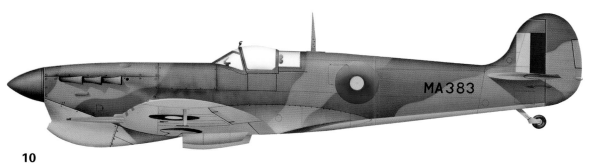

10
Spitfire VC MA383 of Sqn Ldr A N Constantine, No 136 Sqn, Baigachi, India, 10 October 1943

11
Spitfire VC JG807/UP-P of Flt Lt R D Vanderfield, No 79 Sqn RAAF, Vivigangi and Kiriwina, New Guinea, July-December 1943

12
Spitfire VC A58-254/QY-F of Flt Lt A P Goldsmith, No 452 Sqn RAAF, Strauss, Northern Territory, 10 January 1944

13
Spitfire VC A58-220/QY-R of Flg Off J H E Bisley, No 452 Sqn RAAF, Strauss, Northern Territory, 13 January 1944

14
Spitfire VC MH300/KW-S of Flg Off P G Louis, No 615 'County of Surrey' Sqn, Dohazari, India, 16 January 1944

15
Spitfire VC MA292/KW-D of Flg Off S L E Weggery, No 615 'County of Surrey' Sqn, Dohazari, India, 16 January and 26 April 1944

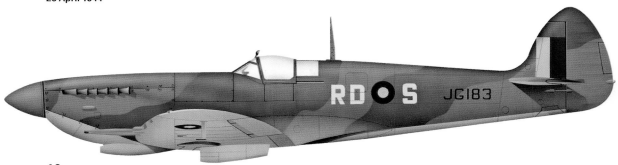

16
Spitfire VIII JG183/RD-S of Flg Off C V Bargh, No 67 Sqn, Alipore, India, 29 February 1944

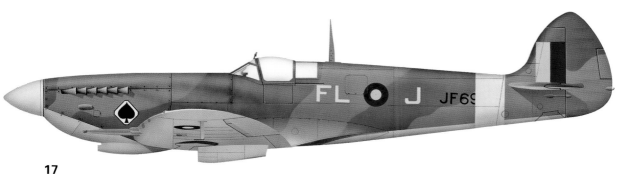

17
Spitfire VIII JF698/FL-J of Sqn Ldr W M Whitamore, No 81 Sqn, 'Broadway' strip, Burma, 13 March 1944

18
Spitfire VIII JF835/UM-T of Sqn Ldr M R B Ingram, No 152 Sqn, Chittagong, India, 6 April 1944

19
Spitfire VIII MT567/HM-B of Flt Sgt R W Cross, No 136 Sqn, Wanjing, India, 8 April 1944

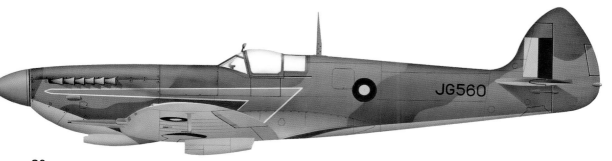

20
Spitfire VIII JG560 of Wg Cdr F R Carey, AFTU, Armada Road, India, April-November 1944

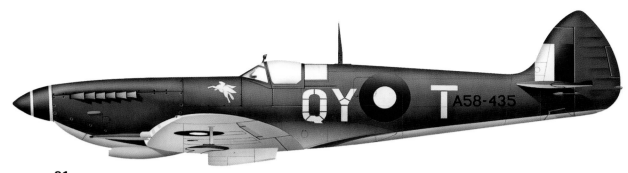

21
Spitfire VIII A58-435/QY-T of Flt Lt W R Cundy, No 452 Sqn RAAF, Sattler, Northern Territory, July-September 1944

22
Spitfire VIII A58-354/DL-V of Sqn Ldr S Linnard, No 54 Sqn, Livingstone, Northern Territory, August-September 1944

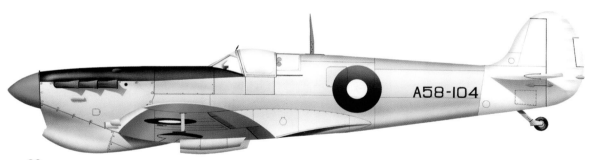

23
Spitfire VC A58-104 of Sqn Ldr W J Storey, CGS, Cressy, Victoria, September 1944-September 1945

24
Spitfire VIII A58-379/ZF-Z of Sqn Ldr E P W Bocock, No 549 Sqn, Strauss, Northern Territory, 1 October 1944

25
Spitfire VC A58-252/UP-A of Flt Lt L S Reid, No 79 Sqn RAAF, Momote, New Guinea, 4 October 1944

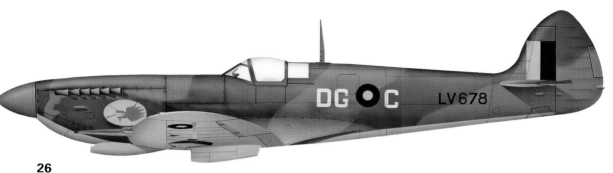

26
Spitfire VIII LV678/DG-C of Flg Off A H Witteridge, No 155 Sqn, Palel, India, September-November 1944

27
Spitfire VIII A58-514/ZP-Q of Flt Lt A Glendinning, No 457 Sqn RAAF, Sattler, Northern Territory, late 1944

28
Spitfire VIII MD215/DG-Y of Sqn Ldr J H Lacey, No 155 Sqn, Palel, India, 7-8 November 1944

55

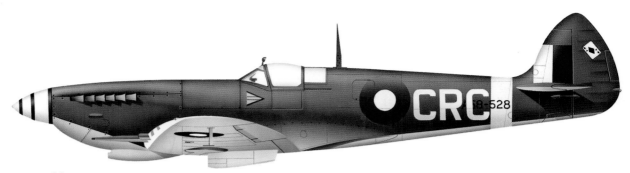

29
Spitfire VIII A58-528/CRC of Wg Cdr C R Caldwell, No 80 Fighter Wing, Morotai, Netherlands East Indies, January-March 1945

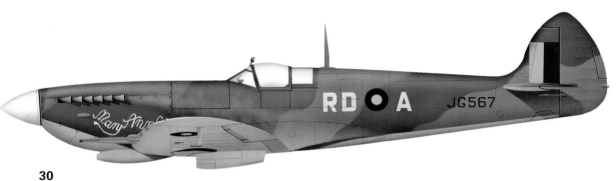

30
Spitfire VIII JG567/RD-A of Sqn Ldr R W R Day, No 67 Sqn, Maunghnama, Burma, 9 January 1945

31
Spitfire VIII A58-602/RG-V of Wg Cdr R H M Gibbes, No 80 Fighter Wing, Tarakan, Borneo, January-April 1945

32
Spitfire VIII MT879/UM-F of Flg Off L A Smith, No 152 Sqn, Sinthe, Burma, March 1945

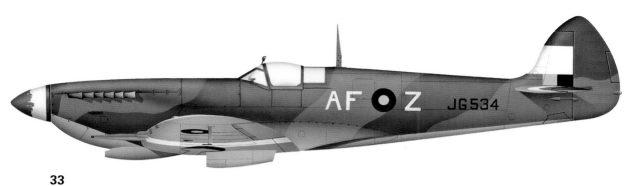

33
Spitfire VIII JG534/AF-Z of Flg Off J R Andrew, No 607 'County of Durham' Sqn, Mingaladon, Burma, 10 June 1945

34
Spitfire VIII MT904/AF-X of Sqn Ldr C O J Pegge, No 607 'County of Durham' Sqn, Mingaladon, Burma, June-July 1945

35
Spitfire VIII MV483/DG-A of Sqn Ldr A G Conway, No 155 Sqn, Thedaw, Burma, late July 1945

36
Spitfire VC A58-248/SH-Z of Sqn Ldr K E James, No 85 Sqn RAAF, Pearce, Western Australia, July-August 1945

Seen on standby at Palel in June 1944, Spitfire VIII MD373/KW-F was regularly flown by Flg Off H B Chatfield throughout the period. He claimed three Spitfire kills with No 615 Sqn, but none in this particular aircraft (*H Costain*)

up to 10,000 ft, before diving from out of the sun at the enemy aircraft. Two of the 'Oscars' were damaged. Sections from Nos 81 and 615 Sqns that had also been ordered off then joined in, and Lt J G White of the former unit claimed a probable – his Spitfire was damaged, however. No 615 Sqn's CO, Sqn Ldr McCormack, attacked what he reported as an all black 'Oscar' with a lightning flash, and he too was also credited with a probable.

Shortly after 0700 hrs on 29 May, 30+ Ki-43s appeared over Imphal on a sweep, prompting No 607 Sqn to scramble its Spitfire VIIIs – the unit failed to make contact. No 615 Sqn enjoyed better fortune, however, with its pilots claiming four 'Oscars' damaged. Overwhelmed by the Japanese fighters, two pilots had their Spitfire VCs badly shot up and Flt Sgt H K Young was killed (in MA383).

By now the weather was progressively worsening due to the imminent onset of the monsoon season, although this time its arrival would not mark the end of the fighting. The situation in the Imphal valley was becoming increasingly desperate for the Japanese, and as the Allied position gradually improved, so the enemy slowly began to retreat.

It was at this time too that No 152 Sqn moved from Comilla to the forward base at Palel so as to better perform long-range escort work, for which purpose its aircraft were equipped with belly tanks. In the wake of the transfer on 31 May, one of the unit's pilots noted in his diary;

'Moved to Palel, a small all-weather strip at the southern end of the Imphal valley. The valley was encircled by mountains several thousand feet high at its northern end, dropping down to a few hundred feet at Palel, where we all lived in Bashas (grass huts) on the hillside overlooking the strip. Our main problem was to get the aircraft out, and back in again, over the surrounding mountains during the awful monsoon weather.'

The Chindit force that was creating such problems for the enemy well behind the frontline also required constant air re-supply, and escort for these vulnerable Dakota sorties became a high priority for the longer range aircraft of Sqn Ldr Bruce Ingram's No 152 Sqn. One such mission was flown early on 10 June, when he led a dozen Spitfires tasked with escorting a Dakota sent to re-supply troops in the Lake Indawgyi area. Things did not get off to a good start when Ingram's No 2, WO J W Vickers, lost a wheel on take-off – he continued nevertheless. Unfortunately, the weather proved so bad that the Dakota was forced to abandon the mission without dropping its precious cargo, and Vickers had to make a wheels-up landing upon his return to base.

Five days later, No 615 Sqn's Spitfire VCs repeated the sortie to the same area, but on the return flight in heavy cloud three pilots (Plt Off A Hyde and Flt Sgts E Kennedy and J McKay) were killed when their Spitfires crashed.

Yet despite the poor weather, the JAAF was still attempting to support retreating Japanese troops on the ground. Shortly before noon on 17 June, No 170 Wing leader Wg Cdr Pat Lee scrambled with a section of No 607 Sqn aircraft that in turn joined up with patrolling Spitfires from Nos 81 and 615 Sqns. Lee was the first to spot intruding Ki-43s, and after calling a brief warning, he dived on one and saw his fire hit the fighter's cockpit. Quickly engulfed in flames, the 'Oscar' rolled over and dived into a paddy field. Moments later, Lee

Wing Leader of No 170 Wing, which included both Nos 81 and 136 Sqns, in mid-1944 was Wg Cdr Pat Lee, who shot down two Ki-43s on 17 June (*N Franks*)

spotted a second 'Oscar' flying low over the Shuganu valley. Diving on the aircraft, he fired at full deflection and hit the Ki-43 near the wing root – it too crashed.

No 607 Sqn then joined in the fight when Sqn Ldr Davies found more 'Oscars' in the general area. He despatched one of them and Flg Off Horace Taylor got another, while other pilots claimed three more as probables. Then it was No 615 Sqn's turn, and Flg Off Kevin Gannon (in MA654) was soon in the thick of the action;

'Dived from 13,000 ft to 8000 ft and attacked one enemy aircraft from astern and above with a short burst, closing from 400 to 300 yards. The enemy aircraft, which was flying south at about 6000 ft, turned quickly to starboard. Fired a long burst from dead astern, closing from 200 to 50 yards, and saw pieces fly off the enemy aircraft. The pilot attempted to bail out but his parachute got caught in the tail. The enemy aircraft, now flaming from its starboard wing, rolled onto its back and crashed near Teinkaya.'

Gannon's wingman, Flt Sgt Bert Chatfield, was also successful in claiming his third victory, having initially attacked the same aircraft as Gannon but without hitting it. Chatfield recalled;

'Immediately afterwards, I attacked another "Oscar" flying south down the valley at 500 ft. Fired two short bursts and one long burst from astern, closing from 300 to 100 yards. Pieces flew off the tail and flames spouted out from the starboard wing root. The enemy aircraft dived down in flames to starboard and crashed.'

The Spitfire units claimed six destroyed, and records for the 50th and 204th Sentais confirm that five Ki-43s were lost. One of the pilots shot down was 16-victory ace Sgt Maj Tomesaku Igarashi of the 50th Sentai. This proved to be the final enemy fighter sweep over Imphal prior to the onset of the monsoon season.

It was at around this time that another ace joined the ranks of No 607 Sqn, when Plt Off James Andrew arrived. He had claimed six victories over Sicily and Italy during the previous 12 months.

Escort sorties for Dakota transports and Vengeance dive-bombers (particularly those supporting the Chindit force) continued throughout this period. One such mission to the Lake Indawgyi area on 21 June saw

No 152 Sqn being led by unit CO, Sqn Ldr Bruce Ingram. Upon the squadron's return to Palel, the young ace crashed-landed. Suffering a broken nose and a badly lacerated face, Ingram was taken to a field hospital in Imphal, where he contracted malaria and then tetanus. Despite the best efforts of the medical staff, he died on 11 July. Ingram's loss was greatly felt by his squadron.

Ironically, 24 hours after his accident, the 74-day siege of Imphal was finally lifted when the 2nd and 5th Divisions met on the road to Kohima, to the north of Imphal, thus marking the beginning of the end for the Japanese in India. The remnants of the enemy's once mighty army then began to struggle back into Burma, starving, diseased and disorganised. More than 53,000 Japanese troops had perished during the offensive, and the Allies had also paid a heavy price as well, losing some 17,000 men.

The air operations in the Manipur province and the Arakan eventually saw the Allies achieve a degree of dominance over the JAAF. Much of this could be credited to better training and preparation, but the official history of the air war in Burma singles out one RAF officer as being primarily responsible for countering improved enemy tactics;

'The man chiefly responsible was that experienced pilot, Frank Carey, promoted to group captain. He was the "backroom boy" of the Burma victory in air supremacy, the man whose refresher courses in gunnery and tactics at his school near Calcutta produced some of the most ingenious fighter pilots of the war.'

A 28-kill veteran of the Battles of France and Britain, and also the 'darks days' in Burma in early 1942, Carey was the CO of the Air Fighting Training Unit at Armada Road.

Spitfire VIII JG606/KW-H of No 615 Sqn awaits its next sortie during July 1944. On the 15th of that month, just after the siege of Imphal had been lifted, JG606 was flown on a troop strafing sortie by Flg Off 'Nappy' Carroll, who by then had made five claims, including two destroyed (via N Franks)

The man credited with much of the success enjoyed by RAF fighter pilots in Burma was 28-kill ace Wg Cdr Frank Carey, who ran the Air Fighting Training Unit at Armada Road, in northeastern India. He is seen here with his personal Spitfire VIII JG560, which boasted a red marking on both sides of its fuselage so that his students could spot him in the air! (F R Carey)

His team of experienced instructors included such successful aces as Flt Lt J H 'Ginger' Lacey. Of his unit, Carey wrote;

'I was asked to gather together a few experienced pilots who had operated against the Japanese and form a small training team. The team and I worked out a suitable training syllabus to get things going. Very quickly, after starting with a few chaps from each squadron, they went back to pass the details on to the other pilots.

One technique his team taught was the rolling attack to counter the agile enemy fighters, as Carey described. 'You have a good view of your target. It is easy to assess the line of flight as the ground helps you. Your aircraft is a comfortable platform for shooting'.

The official history gave this valediction on Carey's influence. 'It was said that a remarkable proportion of enemy fighters brought down were destroyed by pilots listening to the echo of Carey's voice and obeying his teaching'.

MOVE INTO BURMA

Soon after the siege was lifted the monsoon arrived, bringing with it thick cloud, torrential rain and generally poor weather, in spite of which operations continued. As well as the battles around Imphal, the actions of the Chindits and US-led Chinese forces in the north forced the enemy to begin a slow withdrawal. The fanatical Japanese were by no means finished, however, as illustrated one night in early July when a number of them stole into Palel and destroyed two of No 152 Sqn's Spitfires (JF283 and JF284).

Early July saw the withdrawal from Imphal of some of those units that had endured the siege. On the 6th, the long serving No 607 Sqn left for Baigachi, and a well-deserved rest – it was replaced at Imphal Main by No 152 Sqn. During its time at Imphal No 607 Sqn had claimed 12 aircraft destroyed, 9 probables and 26 damaged. Also arriving at the Arakan front with Spitfire VIIIs in early July were the recently equipped Nos 67 and 273 Sqns, the latter replacing the veteran No 136 Sqn.

Having defeated the JAAF in northern Burma, RAF fighter units were now free to conduct more offensive work in support of the ground forces.

The pilot of Spitfire VIII JG183/RD-S of No 67 Sqn eases into a 'three-pointer' at Comilla in July 1944. Flg Off 'Ketchil' Bargh had flown the unit's first Spitfire scramble in this aircraft on 29 February, and the fighter was wrecked in early 1945 when a bomb fell off it when landing (*H Levy*)

One such operation saw No 615 Sqn use its new Spitfire VIIIs to mount a strafing attack on 400 enemy troops near Sadu. Four-aircraft 'Rhubarbs' of the supply routes along the River Chindwin were also flown on an increasingly regular basis, with sampans often being sunk.

At the beginning of August, No 81 Sqn, after a successful, if at times traumatic, period of operations, flew its final sorties over Burma before withdrawing to Minneriya on the 10th for a deserved rest. That same day, No 615 Sqn was also withdrawn to Baigachi, although under more harrowing circumstances. During its transit sortie from Palel, the unit encountered a severe monsoon storm and eight aircraft crashed with the loss of four pilots, including the CO, Sqn Ldr D W McCormack. WO C M G Watson, who survived this tragic incident, recalled the ill-fated flight in Norman Franks' volume, *The Air Battle of Imphal*;

'It was the weather that dealt the squadron the cruellest blow. The squadron was transferred to Baigachi for a rest. There were 16 aircraft in close formation. The CO – a very fine CO, but more than a little battle weary after a long period of responsibility – led us into a series of "cu nimbs", each one rougher than the last. Finally, we entered one which was thick and black and extremely turbulent. Suddenly we hit a fantastic up current which lifted the whole squadron up as though a gigantic balloon had shot up through a flock of birds. Somehow, I seemed to have an overall view of everything before I was turned upside-down and went into a shrieking dive.

'I was flying No 3 to the CO in the centre of the formation. I saw his No 2 (Australian WO A Chapple) shoot up and chew off the CO's tail with his prop. Needless to say, both men were killed. In all, we lost eight aircraft and four pilots.'

Four days later (14 August), No 155 Sqn, after a period of defensive duties near Calcutta, moved to Palel to replace No 615 Sqn. The unit flew its first 'op' from here on the 15th when it escorted Hurricane fighter-bombers into Burma. Further to the south in the Arakan, Nos 67 and 273 Sqns had started flying combined strikes with US and Indian units against targets in the Mayu valley.

Although there were still occasional encounters, the JAAF in Burma was now a mere shadow of its former self, and thus air combats soon became something of a rarity. The emphasis on offensive work did, however, result in a consequent increase in losses to ground fire, and when a No 152 Sqn pilot was killed when he crashed into the target he was attacking, HQ No 221 Group issued the instruction that 'a few scruffy Japs were not worth the loss of a pilot and an aircraft'.

Towards the end of August Allied intelligence reported that 36 Ki-44 'Tojo' fighters had been seen on the airfield at Onbauk, so No 152 Sqn, led by its new CO, Maj W H Hoffe SAAF, mounted a strafing attack. It was disappointed to find only one aircraft at the base, however, and this was promptly destroyed by WO Eels.

The beginning of September saw a gradual improvement in the weather, although it remained unpredictable and continued to severely hamper air activity. In the Arakan, however, there was a resumption of fighting around Buthidaung, and on the 4th the very last Japanese troops were finally ejected from Indian soil. Slowly, overwhelming Allied might had begun to exert itself.

Towards the end of the month there was a brief upsurge in activity when, on 24 September, No 152 Sqn scrambled a section after a Japanese reconnaissance aircraft. The unit's records described the event as follows;

'After an uneventful day, a scramble was ordered at 1700 hrs and four aircraft took off, one of which soon had to return to base. An exciting chase followed in which the aircraft were well controlled from the ground. Eventually, Flg Off P Ardeline, closing in from the sun on a Jap Army Type 01 "Dinah", shot it down in flames after only two short bursts. The approach from the sun evidently allowed Flg Off Ardeline to get into a firing position without the knowledge of the Jap pilot, who could never have known what had happened.'

The following day another 'Dinah' appeared, as No 155 Sqn pilot Flg Off Albert 'Witt' Witteridge explained to the author;

'We were scrambled against two high level bogies. I spotted one at 26,000 ft, heading home to Burma. We chased it 100 miles at 405 mph TAS (true air speed) and eventually got within firing range. Strikes were seen on the fuselage and inboard wing and some return fire was observed. After a second burst the "Dinah" began to disintegrate, and it came down near Pinlebu. I initially shared the victory with my No 2, Flt Sgt Pete Lunnon-Wood, but I was subsequently given overall credit for the claim.'

Witteridge had been flying his assigned Spitfire VIII (LV678/DG-C) on this mission, the aircraft having been decorated with the Chindit badge by his groundcrewman, 'Chiefy' Rodemark, in honour of their XIVth Army colleagues. Rodemark and 'Witt' had made some modifications to their Spitfire, as the latter explained;

'The Spit VIII was probably the best of its type ever. I have 1000 hours on Spits, including flying Griffon-powered marks. The VIII had a stronger mainspar than the IX, a retractable tailwheel and 12 gallons of extra fuel in each wing leading edge. My Spit VIIIC did its 240 hours to major overhaul with no problems. We took off the rear view mirror and removed the outboard machine guns, ballast in the tail, armour plate behind the pilot's seat and the emergency lock. We also polished the wing leading edges. These mods made it quite a boy racer!"

Flg Off 'Witt' Witteridge of No 155 Sqn examines his personal Spitfire VIII LV678/DG-C, which, as well as wearing the Chindit badge on its nose, was also modified to increase its performance. Witteridge claimed a Ki-46 and a Ki-43 destroyed whilst flying this machine. Squadronmate Flt Lt 'Babe' Hunter also downed a 'Dinah' whilst flying LV678 (*A H Witteridge*)

The JAAF's sleek 'Dinahs' were also active over Bengal too, and during the early afternoon of 2 October Flt Lt L S Laughton and Flg Off E P Bruce of No 273 Sqn were scrambled after a bogey to the west of Chittagong. Within minutes of taking off Bruce sighted the Ki-46 above him and to starboard. As the Spitfires approached the intruder, it turned away and dived to low level. The chasing pilots gradually closed the range and identified it as a 'Dinah'. Closing from the right, they saw their combined fire hit its starboard wing. The Ki-46 then pulled up to about 200 ft, and as it climbed Laughton came in from astern and opened fire once again. As he broke away, large pieces fell off the Japanese aircraft, which then blew up. 'Needless to say, there were terrific parties in all the squadron messes in the evening to celebrate the squadron's first kill', recalled the unit records.

Five days later, New Zealander Flt Lt L T 'Babe' Hunter of No 155 Sqn shot down yet another 'Dinah'. Flying Witteridge's aircraft, he had intercepted the Ki-46 some 60 miles to the southeast of Tamu at 29,000 ft, and as it lost height one of the crew was seen to bail out.

The beginning of October also saw an organisational change when the RAF's tactical wings were renumbered, with No 165 Wing becoming No 903 Wing, for example. At Chittagong, No 902 Wing controlled the Spitfire-equipped Nos 67 and 273 Sqns, among other units.

ACROSS THE CHINDWIN

During October the British Army was to cross the Chindwin in some strength at three points, after which it began to concentrate for an advance down the Shwebo Plain. By the end of the month Army engineers had hacked an airstrip out of thick jungle at Tamu, near the northern end of the long Kabaw valley, and on the 29th No 152 Sqn moved in. It duly became the first RAF squadron to be based in Burma since the retreat of 1942.

Little had been seen of JAAF fighters for some time, but on 4 November Allied intelligence warned the Spitfire units that a mass attack was likely the following day. And so it transpired, for at dawn a dozen Ki-43s from the 64th Sentai attacked Palel. 'Witt' Witteridge was one of those involved, and he vividly described the subsequent events to the author;

'We scrambled after a dozen fighters nearing the base just before dawn. We had difficulty joining up in the bad light, but some had sightings. I saw one near Palel strip, but my No 2, WO C W Gentry, had not managed to follow me and subsequently went missing. The enemy aircraft was an "Oscar II", and with height advantage, I bounced it. However, as I closed into range its pilot did a violent turn into the attack and I couldn't keep deflection on, so I pulled up to regain height. As I did so the Jap stood on his tail and fired at me, but missed. This performance went on for some time before I worked out the best way to clobber him. Letting the speed fall back to near the stall whilst still about 2000 ft above him, I dropped down with a rush at low speed, turned well inside the Jap, fired my weapons and then banged on full throttle so as to re-establish my speed advantage. Moments later the "Oscar II" hit a hillside ten miles from Palel.

'We had a look at the wreck on the ground with some Gurkhas – it was riddled with holes, and it was a wonder that it stayed up as long as it did.'

'Witt's' final victory was not No 155 Sqn's only success that morning, for against the loss of WO Gentry, WO W B Parker also shot a Ki-43 down and WOs C W Elliot and R Willdey got in long bursts that each damaged an 'Oscar'. Witteridge was congratulated on his victory by none other than 27-kill ace Sqn Ldr 'Ginger' Lacey, who was attached to No 155 Sqn pending his posting to No 17 Sqn as its new CO.

Also alerted was No 152 Sqn at Tamu, and among those who scrambled was Flg Off Len Smith. He claimed a Ki-43 shot down (and a second one damaged) to take his final wartime tally to 5.5 kills, this being his only victory over the Japanese. Assigned to No 152 Sqn in early 1943, Smith had claimed three German and 1.5 Italian fighters destroyed in the Mediterranean in 1943. Squadronmate WO J W Vickers described the action in his diary;

'At sparrow-fart on 5 November, all strapped in and ready, we were off and up at the merest glimmer of "first light". However, no mass attack came, just a few Jap "Oscars" coming in low to be met by A Flight's Flg Off L A Smith, who promptly added One Confirmed and One Damaged to his score. This kill earned Smithy a well-deserved DFM.'

Three days later the JAAF reappeared when 64th Sentai Ki-43s that were out on a ground attack mission spotted some Dakotas and claimed four of them shot down. A fifth one was destroyed a short while later by Cpl Ikeda, and although No 152 Sqn was scrambled to intercept the Japanese fighters, they arrived on the scene too late to catch any of them. As a result of these losses, the Spitfire squadron provided escorts for the Dakotas on 9 November, and the enemy fighters turned away from the transports once they saw them.

By now, with Allied forces pushing further south into Burma, most of the action was beyond the range of the Spitfire units based in Assam.

During November 'Ginger' Lacey familiarised himself with the area whilst attached to No 155 Sqn. He flew his last sortie with the unit on the 21st, when he led WO Elliot on an uneventful patrol of Yasagyo. Lacey then joined No 17 Sqn at Sapam. Upon his arrival he noted;

No 17 Sqn replaced its Hurricane IICs with Spitfire VIIIs in Ceylon in March 1944, and eventually moved to Assam in November 1944. Here, the unit welcomed Sqn Ldr 'Ginger' Lacey as its new CO. JG614/G was one of No 17 Sqn's aircraft, and it is seen here at Vavuniya awaiting the addition of unit codes (*P R Arnold Collection*)

'Morale on the squadron is excellent, although it appears to have spent too much time in Ceylon and has become a little stale. This staleness disappeared almost immediately, and we are now expectantly awaiting the appearance of the first Jap aircraft of No 17's second Far East operational tour.'

In the event it was to be 1945 before Lacey's wish came true. Typical of the sorties flown by the unit during this period was the 11 December operation that saw No 17 Sqn's Spitfires escort C-46 transports during a routine supply mission. That same day further south, No 273 Sqn's Spitfires were scrambled from Cox's Bazaar when a JAAF sweep was detected approaching the Japanese stronghold of Akyab. In the subsequent 'bounce' WO I H S Pelling and Plt Off F W Collard each damaged an 'Oscar', although WO G R Bullion was shot down during the course of the combat. The Ki-43s had been trying to attack elements of XV Corps, which, spearheaded by the 25th Indian and 81st West African Divisions, began to advance down the pestilential Kaladan and Kalapanzin valleys the very next day.

On 18 December, it was with some satisfaction that Sqn Ldr Lacey's No 17 Sqn returned to Burma, from where it had been ejected in March 1942. Having moved to Taukkyan, it started flying patrols over the Kalewa bridgehead that spanned the Chindwin.

It was at this time too that a further unit reorganisation saw the RAF's No 221 Group allocated to support the XIVth Army in its drive through central Burma, while No 224 Group helped XV Corps push south along the west coast – each group included Spitfire squadrons. On 20 December IV Corps captured Wuntho, and three days later the 36th Division took Tigyaing. On Christmas Day Len Smith and his squadronmates from No 152 Sqn flew patrols over the expanding Kalewa bridgehead, with No 907 Wing's wing leader, Wg Cdr R F Riggall, regularly flying with the squadron. Sqn Ldr Bob Day, who had achieved four successes with No 81 Sqn, received a well deserved promotion on 25 December when he took over command of No 67 Sqn.

January 1945 saw the Allied advance really beginning to gain momentum, with the enemy finally yielding Akyab. The seizure of this vital port city meant that amphibious operations could now be mounted from here along the Burmese coast. Japanese forces opposing the XIVth Army now also began to pull back south of the Irrawaddy.

The personal aircraft of most Wing Leaders carried their initials as was their privilege. JF902 of Wg Cdr Robert Riggall (Wing Leader of No 907 Wing) was no exception, the fighter being photographed at Akyab during 1945 (*R H Riggall*)

Most of the Japanese pilots shot down by No 67 Sqn on 9 January were killed, but Maj Toyoki Eto, a 12-victory ace of the 64th Sentai, survived the one-sided action by crash-landing his Ki-43 at Myebon and making contact with Japanese troops in the area (*via B Cull*)

Yet another Spitfire squadron entered the fray at this point when No 8 Sqn Indian Air Force commenced operations from Cox's Bazaar.

The fall of Akyab drew an immediate Japanese response when, on the 9th, Maj Koki Kawamoto led seven of the 50th Sentai's new Ki-84 'Franks' on the unit's first attack on Allied shipping. They were covered by 28 Ki-43s from the 64th Sentai, led by veteran aces Majs Hideo Miyabe and Toyoki Eto. As the 'Franks' began their attack shortly before 1400 hrs, five Spitfires from No 67 Sqn (which had just moved down to Akyab) took off, led by Sqn Ldr Day, to counter the threat.

Prior to the RAF fighters engaging the JAAF fighters, Eto led four Ki-43s in an attack on a Sea Otter from No 292 Sqn that just happened to be in the wrong place at the wrong time. They forced the amphibian down with its top wing on fire and the gunner dead. They were then spotted by Day's section, however, which dived after the 'Oscars' and intercepted them off Myebon at 4000 ft. Caught cold, all five Ki-43s were claimed destroyed. Eto's three wingmen, Sgts Takashi Imajin, Hideo Tamazuki and Ryuzo Yamamoto, were killed, while Eto himself crash-landed at Myebon and made contact with Japanese ground forces.

During the melee two of the 'Oscars' fell to Bob Day, who thus became the last Spitfire pilot to become an ace over Burma – he was awarded a DFC soon afterwards. Two others were credited to Flt Lt Simpson and the last one to WO McQuarrie. In a press interview staged immediately after this engagement, New Zealander Clyde Simpson gave the following account of his victories;

'They were going like fury back to their base. I gave one a long burst and he started to burn, finally crashing into a hill. Then I saw a Jap on the tail of one of our Spits. He didn't see me coming and gave me a wide-open shot. I got him fair and square in the belly and he went straight down.'

The following day XIVth Army troops occupied Ye-U, although 'Oscars' of the 64th Sentai still remained active over the front. Indeed, when the 19th Indian Division crossed the Irrawaddy north of Mandalay on 18 January, the JAAF participated in a brilliant diversionary attack that saw the enemy rush reinforcements up to eliminate this new bridgehead. Supporting the troops on the ground, some 28 Ki-43s flew highly effective strafing attacks on the crossings. Further south, the landings on Ramree Island went ahead on the 21st, and once again enemy fighter-bombers attempted to interfere with the shipping offshore. However, on this occasion they were spotted by Spitfires from No 67 Sqn, which dived on them and successfully broke up the attack.

These aerial engagements were very much the exception to the rule, as it was offensive operations in support of troops on the ground that predominated. Typical of the latter was a 'Rhubarb' to Mandalay flown

The last pilot to become an ace flying the Spitfire over Burma was No 67 Sqn's CO, Sqn Ldr Bob Day (right), who, in a brief but violent combat off Akyab on 9 January, shot down two Ki-43s to reach the elite status. Here, he is being congratulated in front of his aircraft immediately after the mission by Wg Cdr R E Drake (*Squadron Records*)

Also claiming two victims in the fight on 9 January was Flt Lt Clyde Simpson RNZAF, who was flying JG199 in which he is posing. These were his only victories (*Squadron Records*)

by Flg Off Don Rathwell, who was now serving with Lacey's No 17 Sqn;

'Took the course Mandalay to Thazi for possible offensive action. Southeast of Thazi a concentration of 50 loaded bullock carts facing northeast was strafed and more than half of them damaged.'

Lacey himself strafed Japanese bunkers a few days later. At the beginning of February he led his squadron across the Chindwin to Ywadon as the battle for central Burma reached its climax. Through some brilliant tactical work, Allied forces outflanked the enemy and drove on to Meiktila, all but isolating the powerful Japanese garrison at Mandalay in the process.

10 February saw the start of a flurry of air action when No 67 Sqn claimed another success over Ramree Island in the form of a Ki-46 downed by Australian Flt Lt Hickey and Flt Sgt J L Ellington. Two days later, the 20th Division crossed the Irrawaddy west of Mandalay, while further west the main assault took place. The vital rail and road junction at Meiktila was the key Allied target. Advancing out of the jungle into more open territory, British and Indian troops were now able to take full advantage of their armour and mobility. Despite bitter Japanese resistance, the enemy could not halt the crossing of the mighty Irrawaddy River.

On 14 February Don Rathwell had a peculiar combat during an early patrol near Ywadon when he forced down a radial-engined aircraft that he thought was a Harvard, albeit in Japanese camouflage. This claim was not included in his total. Another 'Dinah' fell to the guns of No 152 Sqn near Mandalay the next day, while on the 17th WO J W Vickers and Flt Sgt E 'Lofty' Unstead each destroyed an 'Oscar II'. The following afternoon Plt Off Bob Connell shot down what he thought was a J1N 'Irving', although it was in fact Lt Hono's Ki-46 'Dinah' from the 81st Sentai.

On the morning of 19 February, during a busy day over the Irrawaddy bridgehead, No 152 Sqn had several brushes with intruding 'Oscar IIs' that resulted in several claims being made. No 17 Sqn was also involved, with 'Ginger' Lacey leading WO Sharkey on a patrol of the Mandalay

Commander of No 906 Wing was Gp Capt Don Finlay, who had achieved six victories in Europe prior to being posted to Burma (*via C F Shores*)

A 40 mm Bofors gun provides protection from attack as No 17 Sqn Spitfire VIII 'YB-M' is serviced at Sapam. Canadian ace Flg Off Don Rathwell was flying this aircraft on 14 February 1945 when he attacked a radial-engined aircraft that he later thought might have been a Harvard, although this would appear to be unlikely (*via J D R Rawlings*)

area at 0725 hrs. Fifty minutes later Sharkey spotted a formation of 'Oscars' and Lacey made a rolling attack on the No 2 aircraft of the last section, reporting afterwards;

'The enemy aircraft started a gentle turn to starboard, and not evasive action. Allowing just over one ring deflection, and from an angle off of about ten degrees, I fired a one second burst at a range of about 150 yards. Three cannon strikes were seen on the cockpit, which disintegrated the hood. The enemy aircraft turned slowly on its back and dived vertically towards the ground. We followed it down to 12,000 ft but broke off when jumped by another "Oscar" from above. This aircraft was evaded by a vertical climb to 18,000 ft. On looking down, I then observed a large cloud of dust and smoke rising from the ground directly below the combat.'

'Ginger' Lacey was credited with destroying the 'Oscar', which was probably the aircraft flown by Sgt Kadokura of the 64th Sentai. His only victory over the Japanese took Lacey's tally to 28 kills. It was also the last over Burma by an ace flying a Spitfire.

PUSH TO RANGOON

As British armour pushed southwards, the JAAF still attempted to intervene, such as on 24 February when 14 Ki-43s tried to attack a British armoured column near Pakokku that was driving towards Meiktila. They were engaged by a pair of No 17 Sqn Spitfires and driven off. Meiktila fell on 5 March, while at Mandalay, three days and nights of savage onslaught by the 19th Division had secured the strategic vantage point of Pagoda Hill, which overlooked the city. The massive mile-square Fort Dufferin was surrounded by British and Gurkha infantry on 15 March, and Mandalay fell five days later following two weeks of sustained air and artillery attack. This heavy fighting had effectively broken the back of Japanese resistance in the area, and in April the drive on Rangoon began.

That same month Nos 17 and 155 Sqns moved via Meiktila to Thedaw and then on to Tennant as they were captured, while No 152 Sqn was transferred down to Magwe, No 273 Sqn to Dabaing and No 607 Sqn to Dwehla, before heading further east to Kalaywa, on the Sittang River. No 615 Sqn, however, had pulled back to India, pending re-equipment with Thunderbolt IIs in June 1945.

Magwe was recaptured in early April, and the irresistible advance by Allied forces on the ground resulted in another brief flurry of air combat. On the 20th, ten Ki-43s from the 64th Sentai, with a top cover of eight Ki-84 'Franks' from the 50th Sentai, attacked advancing armoured units near Pyinmana. They were intercepted by four Spitfires from No 152 Sqn, and in the unit's final air-to-air combat of the war, WO R E Partridge shot down the 'Oscar' flown by Capt Tadayuki Yonekura. He was then attacked by Sgt Masayoshi Higo in

Sqn Ldr 'Ginger' Lacey, CO of No 17 Sqn, smiles for the camera shortly after shooting down a Ki-43 on 19 February 1945 for his 28th, and last, victory. This was also his only success against the Japanese (*via C F Shores*)

WO R E Partridge (right) of No 152 Sqn examines the damage to Sgt Cyril Potter's Spitfire VIII MV406/UM-P after combat with 'Oscars' on 20 April 1945, one of which he had shot down. This aircraft had been flown several times the previous month by 5.5-victory ace Flg Off Len Smith (*via M Goodman*)

Lacey (centre) is flanked by two of his pilots, Plt Off F Irvine (right) and Flg Off Bob Connell (left). The latter claimed the last RAF victory over Burma on 29 April when he shot down a JAAF fighter. He claimed that his victim was a Ki-43, but it was more likely to have been a Ki-84 (*via J D R Rawlings*)

When eight-victory ace Wg Cdr David Cox became the Wing Leader of No 909 Wing in April 1945, he had both Nos 17 and 155 Sqns under his command, and regularly flew with them (*author's collection*)

a Ki-84 and his Spitfire badly damaged, as was the aircraft flown by squadronmate Sgt Cyril Potter.

Four days later, No 17 Sqn engaged 15 Ki-43s that were attacking a large convoy near Toungoo. Flt Lt R S Thompson shot down the fighter flown by Sgt Ishide, who bailed out. Evening up the score, Sgt Derek Crawford was last seen with two 'Oscars' on his tail, and he failed to return to base – his demise, credited to Sgt Konishi, gave the 64th Sentai its last kill in Burma.

Lacey's unit was in action again on 29 April when a four-aircraft dawn patrol led by Flt Lt D C Hindley encountered fighters from the 50th and 64th Sentais attacking a column of British troops in the Toungoo area. Although short of fuel, the four Spitfires engaged the JAAF aircraft and Plt Off Bob Connell claimed a Ki-43 shot down. He had dived through cloud in order to position himself 2000 yards behind the No 2 fighter in the enemy section;

'The "Oscar" pilot made his attack and pulled up left, and as he did so I pulled up inside him and closed to 300 yards. I opened fire at 25 degrees angle off and 400 yards, scoring direct hits on the engine of the No 2 and causing flames to erupt from the port side of the engine cowling. He rolled over and went vertically into the deck with black smoke pouring from him – the fighter blew up on striking the ground.'

As the Ki-43 fell away to its destruction, Connell was attacked by two more fighters and forced to weave violently at treetop level so as to avoid them. Although identified as an 'Oscar', evidence suggests that Connell's victim was in fact the Ki-84 'Frank' flown by Sgt Tomihiro Kondo of the 55th Sentai. Either way, it was the RAF's final air combat victory over Burma. Since re-equipping with Spitfires, No 17 Sqn had claimed five enemy aircraft destroyed and two probables. A little over a week later the RAF's long time adversaries, the 64th Sentai, withdrew from Burma.

On May Day another ace returned to operations when Sqn Ldr Gordon Conway, who had seven victories to his name, arrived at Toungoo to assume command of No 155 Sqn. Allocated Spitfire VIII MV428/DG-G, his first flight was a low level patrol down to Rangoon. Two days later, the Burmese capital fell to an amphibious assault that took place unopposed by the Japanese. The capture of Rangoon coincided with the early arrival of the monsoon.

By the end of May there were thousands of Japanese troops in the Pegu Yomas area of southern Burma attempting to retreat into Siam across the Sittang River. An estimated 15,000 men of Sakurai's army were still lurking in the Irrawaddy valley, however, and the newly formed 12th Army awaited the Japanese breakout with active interest, as RAF units harassed the enemy's retreat. Those who reached the Irrawaddy

Seven-kill ace Sqn Ldr Gordon Conway returned as CO of No 155 Sqn during the final actions against the Japanese. In late July he regularly flew MV483/DG-A on ground attack sorties (*J Geeson*)

Pilots of MT904/AF-X and MT791/AF-P of No 607 Sqn struggle through the mud of a Burmese strip after a sortie against the Japanese pocket in the Sittang bend. MT904 was regularly flown in June-July 1945 by eight-victory ace Sqn Ldr C O J Pegge, whilst fellow ace Flg Off J R Andrew routinely sortied in MT791 (*No 607 Sqn Association*)

were hounded day and night by the Spitfire units, as Sqn Ldr Gordon Conway of No 155 Sqn recalled following just such a mission on 21 June;

'After one of these attacks, we were told that we had killed 60 Japs. The guerrillas had actually seen the remaining soldiers throwing bodies into a chaung. The next day we chased up the surviving party, which amounted to 100 soldiers, and killed a further 56. During this period we ran what we called a "private conflict", and the war for us consisted of No 155 Sqn and the 19th Division against "the rest". Spasmodic sorties of this nature were carried out, and they turned out to be very useful later on, as the boys, who had only previously dropped a few bombs, were by now getting extremely accurate.'

Although the brilliantly fought campaign in Burma was now drawing to its close, losses still occurred, and skill at air combat was of little help in

Above
Flg Off J R Andrew of No 607 Sqn was the last ace lost when flying a Spitfire in Burma, being posted missing on 25 June 1945 (*No 607 Sqn Association*)

Right
No 607 Sqn's CO Sqn Ldr Constantine Pegge (left) discusses the next mission with Wg Cdr R N N Courtney of No 906 Wing (*No 607 Sqn Association*)

Below
No 152 Sqn's distinctive leaping panther marking, seen here on the aircraft assigned to the unit's CO, Sqn Ldr Grant Kerr, at war's end. It was a highly unusual addition for an operational squadron (*M Naydler*)

the lottery of bad weather and ground fire. On 25 June six-kill ace Flg Off James Andrew headed out alone on a ground attack sortie and did not return. He thus became the last ace to die whilst flying a Spitfire in the war against the Japanese. The next day his squadron welcomed fellow ace Sqn Ldr C O J Pegge in from No 131 Sqn as its new CO, and he immediately began flying on operations.

Elsewhere, on 28 June No 17 Sqn began conversion to the Griffon-engined Spitfire XIV – this continued into July. 'Ginger' Lacey remarked at the time that 'there is no marked difference between it and the early Merlin-powered marks, although one is always comfortably aware of the enormous extra power'.

No 607 Sqn flew its last combat mission on 31 July, while No 152 Sqn's final sorties did not come until 8 August. Fighting gradually petered out across much of Burma, but there remained pockets of resistance that saw Spitfire XIVs of No 17 Sqn, supported by Thunderbolt IIs of Nos 42 and 79 Sqns, mount a punitive strike on 29 August. After this mission the war was effectively over for RAF Spitfire units.

IN THE EAST INDIES

While the Spitfires of the RAAF's No 1 Fighter Wing were countering the Japanese raids on Darwin during the early months of 1943, Australian Spitfires were also in action in another theatre where the enemy had been checked, but was by no means defeated – New Guinea.

The RAAF's No 79 Sqn had been formed at Laverton, in Victoria, on 26 April, and as aircraft became available it was equipped with Spitfire VCs. The unit was commanded by Sqn Ldr Alan Rawlinson, who was a highly successful ace with eight victories to his name following his service with No 3 Sqn RAAF in the Middle East in 1940-42. One of his flight commanders was also an ace, C Flight being led by Flt Lt Doug Vanderfield, who had achieved five victories over Malaya flying the Buffalo with No 453 Sqn in 1941-42.

No 79 Sqn conducted work-ups prior to heading to Vivigani, on Goodenough Island in the D'Entracasteaux group, some 15 miles off the eastern coast of New Guinea. Sadly, the move was not without incident, for ten-victory Malta ace Flg Off Vic Brennan was killed in a landing accident at Garbutt, in Queensland, on 13 June – his aircraft burst into flames when it collided with a second Spitfire.

Six days later, and whilst still in transit, No 79 Sqn experienced its first operational scramble from Gurney airfield, at Milne Bay. Flg Off Birch and Sgt Grinnington scrambled to intercept a Japanese reconnaissance aircraft, but they returned to base empty handed. The following day, Vanderfield and Flg Off Hopton were scrambled and climbed to maximum height over Gurney. Again, the JAAF aircraft escaped interception. Upon eventually arriving at Vivigani, No 79 Sqn became part of No 73 Wing, which was commanded by 23-year-old Queenslander Wg Cdr W S 'Woof' Arthur – he too was an ace from the desert fighting.

The wing's other units flew Kittyhawks, so No 79 Sqn's Spitfires were held back for air defence. They were regularly scrambled whilst performing this mission, with Sqn Ldr Rawlinson leading the unit aloft from Vivigani for the first time (in JG740/UP-U, which soon became his regular mount) on 30 June. This mission, like most others, proved to be uneventful.

'Woof' Arthur flew with No 79 Sqn for the first time at the end of July, and in early August the unit moved forward to Kiriwina, in the Trobriand Islands, under less than ideal conditions. This was the nearest Allied base

The first Spitfire unit to serve in New Guinea was the newly formed No 79 Sqn, under the command of desert ace Sqn Ldr Alan Rawlinson, pictured here at Goodenough Island on 20 July 1943 (*No 79 Sqn RAAF*)

OC C Flight of No 79 Sqn was Flt Lt Doug Vanderfield, who was one of the few pilots to have achieved 'acedom' over Malaya flying the portly Brewster Buffalo in 1941-42 (*No 79 Sqn RAAF*)

Spitfire VC JG74?/UP-U was the mount of Sqn Ldr Rawlinson, who named it *Sweet FA*, just as he had done with his Tomahawks in North Africa. Seen at Vivigani airfield, on Goodenough Island, the Spitfire has Mounts Nimadao and Oiamadawa as a backdrop (*No 79 Sqn RAAF*)

Shortly after No 79 Sqn had moved forward for operations, instructions were received for all fighter aircraft in the Southwest Pacific area to carry white identity markings, as is evident on JG891/UP-G at Kiriwina. Sgt George Gilbert's 'Tasmanian Devil' badge was less official! (*P R Arnold collection*)

to the Japanese fortress at Rabaul, and so the expectation of enemy raiders was high. However, the Spitfire pilots saw no action during the standing patrols that they flew during USAAF Fifth Air Force attacks on Rabaul. Sqn Ldr Rawlinson ruefully recalled, 'There was no enemy reaction to this whole operation – a great disappointment to us. What a let down'.

The following month, another ex-desert ace in the shape of Wg Cdr Gordon Steege assumed the position of Wing Leader, and he too was soon flying No 79 Sqn's thoroughbred Spitfire VCs.

The Allied campaign to oust the enemy from New Guinea was now in full flow, with landings along the north coast. On 16 September Lae fell, soon followed by Salamaua and, on 2 October, Finschhafen, which was captured by troops from the 9th Australian Division. Following these reverses the Japanese became more active, mounting air raids on Goodenough and Kiriwina. This increased aerial action by the JAAF eventually resulted in No 79 Sqn at last getting the opportunity to claim its first success on 31 October. Sgt Ian Callister, who had been scrambled in JG807/UP-P, spotted an aircraft emerging from cloud some two miles north of Kiriwina at about 3000 ft. It then dived away to the north, with Callister in hot pursuit. The latter had soon outstripped his wingman, Flt Sgt Forbes, and gradually he overtook the intruder.

Speculatively opening fire at 800 yards, Callister saw hits on the port wing of the fighter, which he now identified as a Ki-61 'Tony'. The JAAF aircraft began to slow dramatically, allowing Callister to open up with a second burst from about 350 yards. The enemy fighter exploded and crashed into the sea from a height of about 800 ft. No 79 Sqn had at last achieved its first victory, which was duly celebrated back at Kiriwina.

Sadly, Sgt Ian Callister was killed six days later when, during an early morning take-off, his Spitfire collided with the aircraft flown by Wg Cdr 'Woof' Arthur – the latter survived, but was badly burned. Rawlinson, who had been promoted and replaced by Sqn Ldr Max Bott just a few days earlier, took over the wing. No 79 Sqn now also boasted another ace within its ranks, as Flt Lt John Cock had been transferred in from No 54 Sqn at Darwin.

On the 27 November No 79 Sqn flew its first sweep over enemy territory when Sqn Ldr Bott led eight aircraft against targets at Gasmata, on the south coast of New Britain. This mission pointed the

Spitfire VC JG807/UP-P, seen here at Kiriwina, was flown by Sgt Ian Callister on 31 October when he shot down a Ki-61 'Tony' to claim No 79 Sqn's first victory. Sadly, Callister was killed a few days later when he collided with Wg Cdr Arthur. Behind JG807 is ES307/UP-X, which was flown on occasion by Flt Lt Doug Vanderfield (*via A Price*)

Eight-victory ace Wg Cdr 'Woof' Arthur commanded No 73 Wing, and he first flew with No 79 Sqn (in EE836/UP-F) on 29 July 1943. Arthur sortied regularly with the squadron until he suffered terrible burns in a collision with another Spitfire on take-off on 6 November 1943 (*via C F Shores*)

way to the unit's future, and in the process No 79 Sqn became the first Spitfire fighter unit to fly over Japanese territory. The following day the squadron's record book recorded another rare aerial success;

'Flg Off Moore was airborne at 0935 hrs on a test flight when he heard instructions being given by Fighter Sector to "Purple" section. Following these directions, he climbed to 30,000 ft and saw an enemy aircraft directly ahead of him. Opening fire with all guns, Flg Off Moore secured hits on the starboard mainplane and engine. During this first burst his starboard cannon jammed, and during the second burst the port cannon ceased firing. Closing in to 100 yards, Flg Off Moore opened fire with his machine guns. The first burst caused pieces to fly from the starboard mainplane and the starboard engine started to smoke. After three bursts, the enemy aircraft went into a gentle dive to approximately 25,000 ft, at which point the starboard engine caught on fire and the aircraft went into a dive, before plunging into the sea.'

When he landed, 'Arch' Moore received confirmation that his success had been over a Ki-46 'Dinah'. His victory was duly celebrated!

The enemy continued to mount occasional attacks on Kiriwina, including raids on 5 and 20 December. There was a further attack the following day when Flg Off Jim Richards (in A58-104/UP-A) and Plt Off Jim Barrie (in A58-28/UP-M) caught another Ki-61 and shot it down. In the event, this was to be No 79 Sqn's final air combat victory, although offensive sweeps continued. During one such mission on the 28th, a Zero-sen was claimed as having been destroyed on the ground at Gasmata. However, as was to be expected, strafing sorties were not without loss, and Flt Lt Llewellyn Wettenhall was shot down during a sweep of New Britain on the 31st.

January 1944 saw No 79 Sqn adopt a more aggressive stance through the mounting of regular offensive sweeps against enemy installations on New Britain. The unit also routinely flew escort missions for dedicated bombing raids. For example, on 17 January eight Spitfires combined with

Carrying a long-range slipper tank, A58-200/UP-C was photographed on 28 March 1944 with Flt Lt Brinsley at the controls during a Beaufighter escort to the Bismarck Archipelago. By this stage of the conflict there were few airworthy Japanese aircraft left in the area to oppose such missions (*via J D R Rawlings*)

33 Kittyhawks to escort Beauforts that had been sent to attack an enemy camp on the Amgen River near Lindenhafen. This mission was repeated on the 22nd and the 30th.

In late February the Allies launched the invasion of the Admiralty Islands. The RAAF would support this offensive by neutralising the remnants of Japanese air power in central New Britain. No 73 Wing, based at Kiriwina, would garrison Los Negros after the island had been secured. The landings encountered stiff opposition, but eventually the wing's Kittyhawks were transferred in from Momote, followed by No 79 Sqn's Spitfires on 28 March. Three days later, the Allies were in control of the entire Admiralty group. There was not a single aerial engagement throughout the campaign – a clear indication of how completely Japanese air power in New Britain had been neutralised, and of how isolated the enemy fortress at Rabaul had become.

Shortly afterwards, the loss of Sqn Ldr Bott in a take-off accident greatly upset the unit, and his replacement was subsequently afflicted with dengue fever, resulting in Sqn Ldr Stan Galton taking command on 25 June.

During the middle months of 1944, No 79 Sqn had been suffering from depressingly poor serviceability, and between August and October things got so bad that the unit was restricted to training flights only. By this time, one of No 79 Sqn's flight commanders was Flt Lt Len Reid, who had made a large number of claims over Malta, thus inspiring him to name his personal Spitfire *HAL FAR*. On 4 October he had a lucky escape when, taking off for a practice flight in A58-252/UP-A (Sqn Ldr Stan Galton's usual mount), the aircraft blew a tyre and on landing swung off the strip at Momote, slewed into a ditch and turned over. When the aircraft was righted, its back was broken and it was reduced to spares, although Reid emerged from the accident uninjured.

On 9 November (almost a year since the unit had last seen a Japanese aircraft in the air) there was excitement when three IJNAF aircraft carried out a surprise daylight raid on Momote, in spite of the fact that they had been tracked by radar for 25 minutes prior to reaching the airfield! Flt Lt O'Dea and Flg Off Kennare were scrambled, but they failed to intercept the enemy fighters. Sqn Ldr Stan Galton was furious;

'Yes, it was a surprise, but it should not have been so because radar had plotted three approaching aircraft for nearly 25 minutes. For 20 of those I had been airborne at up to 10,000 ft, and the tanker was still refuelling my aircraft when the Zeros dive-bombed and opened up

Flt Lt Len Reid, who had achieved considerable success over Malta, joined No 79 Sqn in mid 1944 (*via B Cull*)

with cannons and machine guns. They made one hurried pass before most of us knew what had happened. The navigational skill of those Japanese pilots, and their daring to attack a base as large and well defended as the Admiralty Islands, had to be respected.'

Len Reid was scrambled the following day against a suspected raid, but to his frustration found nothing.

Parked at Momote, in New Guinea, Spitfire VC A58-252/UP-A was usually flown by unit CO Sqn Ldr Stan Galton. However, on 4 October 1944 Flt Lt Len Reid wrote it off when he burst a tyre on landing and the fighter overturned. Fortunately for Reid, he emerged from the wrecked Spitfire unscathed (*P R Arnold Collection*)

NEW WING

By this time Gp Capt Clive Caldwell had returned to a frontline posting, being appointed CO of No 80 Fighter Wing, which had formed for operations in the Dutch East Indies. On 1 July No 452 Sqn, now flying Spitfire VIIIs, moved to Sattler to serve alongside No 457 Sqn, which was also equipped with Mk VIIIs. They had in turn passed their Darwin air defence duties on to Nos 548 and 549 Sqns.

Over the next few months the wing prepared for operations, having also added the newly promoted desert ace Wg Cdr Bobby Gibbes to its ranks. Caldwell had great respect for the latter, stating 'I was delighted of course in 1944 when he was posted to No 80 Fighter Wing as Wing Commander Flying, to be my second in command and my Deputy Wing Leader'. However, the wing was to be employed in a ground-attack rather than a fighter role, which meant that Caldwell and other successful fighter pilots would have little chance to increase their scores.

As part of the overall preparation for the retaking of the Philippines, Morotai Island, located midway between that archipelago and New Guinea, was occupied on 15 September 1944. A short while later, No 80 Fighter Wing, based around Darwin, was informed that it would eventually move to Morotai as part of the 1st Tactical Air Force. Finally, in December, the RAAF wing began moving to the island to provide support to Australian ground forces. No 452 Sqn arrived early on the 12th, and it had become established there within a week. Further aircraft flew in on the 17th, although the squadron left a detachment back at Noemfoor under Flt Lt Cotton. Gp Capt Caldwell arrived during the afternoon of the 21st.

Operations began the following evening, when patrols were mounted against several intruders that came over – some 11 sorties were flown that night. Caldwell duly led from the front by flying an operational sortie almost every day. The Spitfires were soon in action in their unaccustomed role as nightfighters when, on Christmas Eve, Flg Off Jack Pretty shot down a Ki-45 'Nick' nightfighter in flames over Halmahera. This was Pretty's first victory, and it was also No 452 Sqn's first since moving north of the Equator. The unit's diarist duly waxed lyrical;

'Well, we certainly had the best of all Christmas boxes tonight. There were a number of "red alerts", and then at 2200 hrs two enemy aeroplanes came over the Morotai area. Ack-ack and searchlights engaged the first one, but they did not succeed in stopping him and he dropped his bombs.

Gp Capt Clive Caldwell, CO of No 80 Fighter Wing, stands next to his aircraft, which displays his impressive scoreboard. To his intense frustration, the wing saw little air combat during his time in charge (*P H T Green Collection*)

No 452 Sqn's first victory after moving to the East Indies was claimed by Flg Off Jack Pretty on Christmas Eve 1944, when he shot down a Ki-45 'Nick' nightfighter over Halmahera (*via R C B Ashworth*)

Unfortunately, the ack-ack did not stop to give our boys a chance to shoot down the first one.

'The second one came in immediately afterwards, and Flg Off Jack Pretty attacked it, but it wasn't until he had dived through the flak into the attack that the guns finally ceased firing. He managed to get strikes on the enemy – a "Nick" – and set him on fire. The searchlights lost the enemy then, but Flg Off Pretty was able to see the bandit. In two further attacks he succeeded in destroying him, sending him down in flames into the sea. This was witnessed by many thousands of Allied and Australian troops, and cheers rang out everywhere at the sight.'

Sadly, later that same night another Spitfire pilot went missing whilst on a patrol.

In spite of the major operations ongoing in the Philippines, for political reasons the Australians concentrated on the Netherlands East Indies. No 80 Fighter Wing was tasked with maintaining a constant assault on bypassed garrisons so as to neutralise and destroy the enemy in the Celebes, Cerau, Ambon and the Halmaheras. The dangers associated with flying against a cruel and determined enemy were considerable, and on 13 January 1945 Flt Lt Mac Stevenson of No 452 Sqn was captured when he was forced to ditch on a reef close to shore following a strike on Ternate Island. He subsequently died in captivity on Halmahera after being tortured by the Japanese.

Soon afterwards, No 457 Sqn's Spitfires arrived at Morotai, from where they became operational again on 10 February when five Spitfires attacked enemy aircraft on Galela strip. The following day, the unit escorted a Kittyhawk sweep over Cape Balmoeli. By the end of the month No 457 Sqn had completed 113 operational sorties, destroying three barges and one fuel dump, and making numerous strafing runs on parked aircraft and anti-aircraft batteries. Other tasks included top cover in support of bombing raids and hitting enemy supply barges, motor transport and supply depots throughout the Halmaheras and adjoining areas.

Although of indifferent quality, this rare photograph shows a mixed line-up RAAF Spitfires, Mosquitos and a Beaufighter at Morotai. Note Caldwell's A58-528/CRC, in which he flew his final war sorties (*T Hooton*)

The wing's mission tempo in early 1945 can be gauged through the statistics noted by Gp Capt Clive Caldwell in his logbook – 18 operational sorties in less than three weeks.

No 79 Sqn, which had moved back to Sattler to re-equip with Spitfire VIIIs, began flying in to Morotai at this time, and in early March Wg Cdr Bobby Gibbes arrived to assume the duties of the Wing Leader. He was soon in action when, on the 15th, in company with Flt Lt Galway, he flew a sweep to Cape Salemoeli and strafed some huts. Flt Lt Reid, with Flg Off Nichols, also flew a sweep to northwest Halmaheras and strafed some ground targets. Gibbes sortied with No 79 Sqn again on the 18th, and he continued to see action with the unit through to April, when he was posted back to Australia. Caldwell also flew his final war operation at this time when, on 28 March, he reconnoitred Tarakan in preparation for the Australian landing in Borneo.

On 11 April Len Reid had a narrow escape when, during a dusk strike on Miti on 11 April, his aircraft was hit in the radiator by flak and he bailed out some six miles offshore, spending an uncomfortable night in his dinghy. Fortunate not to have been spotted by the searching Japanese, he was picked up instead by a US Navy PT boat just three miles offshore. Reid's first words upon being rescued were 'That's the worst bloody night I have ever spent'. Two days later, he led another patrol back to Miti, but enemy targets in Halmahera were well defended with light and heavy flak.

FRUSTRATIONS IN DARWIN

Although the last large scale bombing raid on Darwin had taken place in November 1943, there were still occasional encounters between the Spitfires of No 1 Fighter Wing and Japanese reconnaissance aircraft over northern Australia into 1944. However, the general lack of activity now found in this theatre led to the following reflection by seven-kill ace Flt Lt Ron Cundy of No 452 Sqn;

'The monotony of sitting around the flight hut on readiness waiting for the Japs, who never came, was relieved from time to time with line astern chases, battle climbs in squadron formation, shadow shooting and aerobatics. We had some outstanding young aviators who would have made excellent combat pilots but were destined to serve without clashing with enemy aircraft.'

There was some excitement when, in early March 1944, a report of a Japanese carrier group steaming through the Sunda Strait led to speculation of an air strike on Western Australia. No 452 Sqn, led by Sqn Ldr Lou Spence, was duly despatched to Pearce, north of Perth, for a short time until the 'flap' passed, whereupon the unit returned to Livingstone.

In part to relieve the monotony, on 18 April Spitfires from all three squadrons (Nos 54, 452 and 457), escorted by Beaufighters from No

The Wing Leader of No 80 Fighter Wing was the ebullient 12-victory ace Wg Cdr Bobby Gibbes, who, like his CO, Gp Capt Caldwell, became frustrated at the lack of air combat (*via C F Shores*)

As Wing Leader of No 80 Fighter Wing, Wg Cdr Bobby Gibbes flew Spitfire VIII A58-602/RG-V, which also carried his initials and his impressive kill tally (*via C F Shores*)

During the latter part of his time with No 452 Sqn in Darwin, desert ace Flt Lt Ron Cundy flew this immaculate Spitfire VIII A58-435/QY-T, which is seen here at Sattler in July 1944. To Cundy's great frustration he never had the opportunity to engage the Japanese whilst at its controls (*R W Cundy*)

31 Sqn, combined in an attack on a Japanese radio station on Babar Island in the Banda Sea. The strike was led by Gp Capt Peter Jeffrey, and all the aircraft returned safely.

By then two notionally RAF squadrons – Nos 548 and 549 – had been formed, and in mid June they moved to the Darwin area (to Livingstone and Strauss, respectively) to join No 1 Fighter Wing. They took over from the two RAAF units, which on 5 July transferred to the operational control of No 80 Fighter Wing. Then on the 16th, No 549 Sqn, which was commanded by five-victory ace Sqn Ldr Eric Bocock, had its first scramble, but the contact proved to be friendly.

However, at 0730 hrs on 20 July 1944 Lt Kiyoshi Izuka and his observer Lt Hisao Itoh took off from Koepang in their Ki-46 'Dinah' and headed for the Australian mainland. Just over an hour later, the radar

Based at Pearce, in Western Australia, for air defence duties, the Spitfire VCs of No 85 Sqn were delivered to the unit without camouflage in September 1944. This particular aircraft belonged to the CO, Sqn Ldr Ken James, who made a number of claims during his lengthy fighting career (*W J Storey*)

To replace the squadrons transferred to No 80 Fighter Wing in July 1944, two new RAF units were formed at Darwin. One was No 549 Sqn, led by five-victory ace Sqn Ldr Eric Bocock who is seen here standing in the centre of the rear row (*B Wallis*)

station at Cape Leveque detected the intruder, and at 0845 hrs three Spitfires from the No 54 Sqn detachment at Truscott were scrambled. Flt Lt Gossland led off Flt Lt Meakin and Flt Sgt Knapp, and eventually they intercepted the Japanese aircraft at 27,000 ft. Gossland recalled the first sighting in his report;

'I saw a "Dinah" approaching from "three o'clock" about 1500 ft above us, so I tallyhoed and turned to port, which positioned me 700-800 ft astern and below the "Dinah". I started climbing, and as soon as I reached its height it dropped grenade clusters, which burst in groups of 12 to 15 astern and about 500 ft below me.

'By this time I had closed up to 500 ft. I gave a short burst and saw strikes on the port engine, along the fuselage and on the starboard engine. The "Dinah" started burning and went into a very steep dive, with smoke pouring from both engines, right in front of "Red 1", who followed him down, firing at his belly. I saw strikes from his burst on the port wing, which went up in a sheet of flame and shortly after fell off outboard of the port engine. The "Dinah" went into a flat spin, burning furiously. I saw a disturbance in the sea offshore. The port wing was still airborne, and it settled in the sea about half-a-mile from the main crash.'

This was the last Japanese aircraft shot down over Australia during the war. Sadly, just eight days later, Flt Lt Frederick Meakin crashed during a ground attack exercise and was killed. This loss coincided with the arrival of a new CO for No 54 Sqn in the shape of Sqn Ldr Sid Linnard, who had achieved 6.5 victories in the Middle East in 1940-42.

There were still occasional scrambles, such as on 21 August when Flt Lt Dave Glaser led off No 549 Sqn after an unidentified contact, but this again proved friendly. In part to improve morale, on 5 September No 1 Fighter Wing mounted a low level attack on a concealed camp site and various enemy installations at Lingat Bay, on Selaroe Island, just four miles to the east of Selaru airstrip. The 14 Spitfires (four each from Nos 54, 548 and 549 Sqns, each led by their COs, and two from wing HQ, led by the desert ace Gp Capt Peter Jeffrey)

The last Japanese aircraft shot down over Australia was a 'Dinah' brought down by Flt Lts Gossland (centre) and Meakin (right) on 20 July 1944. Sadly, Meakin was killed in an accident soon afterwards (*B Hicks*)

All-silver Spitfire VIII A58-379/ZP-Z was the personal mount of Flt Lt Dave Glaser, although it was flown on occasion by his CO too. It wore a personal 'musketeer' marking beneath the cockpit (*B Wallis*)

A close-up of Flt Lt Dave Glaser's colourful 'musketeer' marking worn on A58-379 (*B Wallis*)

81

were headed by a B-25 for navigation assistance. No 548 Sqn's quartet was led by Sqn Ldr R A Watts, who stated in the squadron's report;

'Airborne at 1055 hrs for rendezvous over Darwin at 1110 hrs. Time on target 1234 to 1239 hrs. Target is 286 miles north from Darwin. No 549 Sqn (Yellow Section) went over target first, followed by No 54 Sqn (Red Section) and then No 548 Sqn (Blue Section). All strafed the target with unobserved results, except smoke, dust haze and fires over target. The Mitchell then dropped 4000 lbs of incendiaries over target area. A heavy ack-ack post near Selaroe strip fired 15-20 rounds at the Mitchell.'

The records also recorded;

'Later we learnt that the mysterious No 4 aircraft in our formation was being flown by Wg Cdr Clive "Killer" Caldwell, the CO of No 80 Fighter Wing, who, learning that something was in the wind, decided to come along. He came along to a certain extent, but got lost on the way and finished up over Babar Island, about 20 degrees off course. There, he waged a private little war of his own, and strafed targets of opportunity.'

Soon after this, all three squadrons concentrated at Darwin, and the leadership of No 1 Fighter Wing changed when Gp Capt B R Walker took command, with Wg Cdr Roy Wilkinson (who had achieved nine victories during the Battle of France) becoming his Wing Leader. On 27 November both men joined No 549 Sqn in a strike aimed at destroying two Japanese radar installations located near Cape Lore, on the south coast of Timor.

Originally, the attacking force was to consist of four Mitchells from No 2 Sqn RAAF and a dozen Spitfires – the latter were to strafe the installations before the Mitchells bombed their targets. However, problems during a refuelling stop meant that only seven Spitfires were able to participate – Walker and Wilkinson, plus five from No 549 Sqn, including the CO Sqn Ldr Eric Bocock. Nonetheless, the strike went ahead, and it was assessed that both targets were destroyed.

Roy Wilkinson, who was first down to strafe, flew his personalised aircraft 'RC-W' for the only time on operations, and the fighters were airborne for almost five hours. At a press briefing afterwards the local Air Officer Commanding said;

'The longest operational flight ever made by Spitfires stands to the credit of the Royal Air Force squadron at Darwin, which smashed the installations on Timor recently. The round trip was more than 850 miles, and there was no loss or damage to the squadron.'

No 54 Sqn remained part of No 1 Fighter Wing through to war's end, and amongst its aircraft at Darwin in late 1944 was Spitfire VIII A58-480/DL-Y (*No 54 Sqn Records*)

The top scoring RAAF pilot against the Japanese was Sqn Ldr Jack Storey, who achieved all of his successes flying Hurricanes with No 135 Sqn in Burma in 1942. He later returned to the Central Gunnery School (CGS) at Cressy to pass on his knowledge (*W J Storey*)

Sqn Ldr Jack Storey arranged for a number of Spitfires to be delivered to the CGS, and A58-104 became his regular mount during his tenure (*W J Storey*)

However, much to the frustration of the three squadrons based around Darwin, it was clear to all that they were in an operational backwater, prompting Eric Bocock to write;

'I am supremely confident that given a job to do, this squadron can do it as well as any other fighter squadron in the Empire Air Forces if it were only given the equipment necessary and a brief period of refresher training.'

His frustration is evident, and it was hardly alleviated with a further attack on Cape Chater on 3 June 1945 against the enemy airstrip there. After refuelling on Melville Island, the Spitfires rendezvoused with four RAAF Liberators over Jaco Island, off the southeast tip of Timor, and the latter then attacked the target – three enemy bombers parked in the open at the airfield. Six of the fighters went in and strafed, with the others, including Bocock and Wilkinson, remaining as top cover. This mission proved to be the swansong for the 'Churchill Wing'.

The squadrons at Darwin were not, however, the only Spitfires flying in Australia, as to feed the operational units based both there and in the East Indies there was a large training organisation in the southern states. Among the instructors serving with these units were a number of aces. For example, Mildura-based No 2 OTU was home to Flt Lt John Waddy, who had claimed 15.5 victories in North Africa, (including three in Spitfires with No 92 Sqn) until mid-1944.

Also serving in a training capacity was the leading RAAF pilot against the Japanese, Sqn Ldr Jack Storey, who had gained eight victories over Burma flying Hurricanes with No 135 Sqn in 1942. Upon his return to Australia in 1944, he had become the chief instructor at the Central Gunnery School at Cressy, where Storey eventually flew Spitfires. He recalled of this time;

'The fighter pilots' section was using out of date methods and had Kittyhawks. I was asked to review the syllabus. I found the Kittyhawks far from perfect and clamoured for Spits, and we duly got eight VCs. Spitfire A58-104 was the aircraft I used mostly. The first time I flew it was on 17 September 1944 in an air test to make sure that it was right when we first got them. My last Spitfire flight was on 7 September 1945. What a pleasure it was to fly this aircraft!'

ENDGAME IN BORNEO

The final campaigns for the RAAF in the Southwest Pacific area were the *Oboe* series of operations aimed at retaking Borneo from the Japanese. The capture of Tarakan, with its oil infrastructure and airfield, was the first priority, and this was entrusted to the 26th Brigade of the 9th Division. The troops went ashore on the morning of 1 May 1945, the landing being effected with little real difficulty. However, a bitter campaign that ran until war's end then ensued against the defenders, who had withdrawn inland.

These operations were controversial, as senior Australian officers felt that *Oboe* contributed little to the defeat of Japan, and that the United States was reluctant to use Australian troops in the re-conquest of the Philippines.

From 28 May, No 79 Sqn, which was part of No 80 Fighter Wing, was to provide the air defence of Morotai. Amongst its other duties, the unit was to continue mounting air attacks on Halmahera alongside No 452 Sqn. The latter unit's Spitfire VIIIs flew combat air patrols after the capture of the airfield at Tarakan, No 452 Sqn then being ordered to take over the base's full day and night air defence. In order to do this, six aircraft had to be kept constantly airborne during daylight hours, with one at night during periods of moonlight. All organised resistance in the area ended on 15 June, at which point the occupation began.

By then Australian troops had landed on Labuan, off the north coast of North Borneo, and on the 17th a dozen Spitfires of No 457 Sqn left Morotai, refuelled at Zamboanga and landed at Palawan. The unit arrived at Labuan the following day, and ground attack missions over Balikpapan commenced on 19 June. There were also a few opportunities for action against the JAAF before the enemy's final surrender.

Sitting on alert at Labuan on the evening of 20 June were Flt Lts J G B Campbell and S G Scrimgeour of No 457 Sqn. Both had previously seen action, with Campbell having destroyed an He 111 and damaged three Ju 87s during his time in North Africa, while Scrimgeour had flown Buffalos in Malaya and later served in Australia.

Sat in A58-620 and A58-631/ZP-V, respectively, at 1835 hrs

Flt Lt J G B Campbell stands on the wing root of A58-620 at Labuan, in Borneo, after he had shared in the destruction of No 457 Sqn's final victory – a Ki-46 – on 20 June 1945 (*via J W Bennett*)

they were scrambled and ordered to head for Toulak Point, as the unit's diary recorded for posterity;

'They were then sent to 12,000 ft in the vicinity of Sipitang, in Borneo. Whilst orbiting this point, a "Dinah" was sighted at "six o'clock" to the section and 1000 ft below them. Flt Lt Campbell made his first attack from below, opening fire at 250 yards and closing to 50 yards. No hits were observed. Flt Lt Scrimgeour made his first attack from slightly below and to the rear of the "Dinah", opening fire at 350 yards and closing to 50 yards. When the attack was broken off, the aircraft's port engine was on fire, with pieces flying from it.

'Flt Lt Campbell then made the second attack from line astern, opening fire from 200 yards and closing to 20 yards, and he was followed in by Flt Lt Scrimgeour, who opened fire at 350 yards and closed to 20 yards. Both pilots obtained hits on the starboard engine, rear Perspex and tail, setting the starboard motor on fire and causing pieces to fly off the tail. The "Dinah" was then seen to crash and explode on the ground five miles southeast of base.'

This was the first Japanese aircraft destroyed by the RAAF over Borneo. After the excitement of this rare air combat success, No 457 Sqn continued with its more usual routine of ground attacks. For example, on 23 June the CO, Sqn Ldr Bruce Watson, took off at 1525 hrs with Flt Lt Scrimgeour and others on an armed reconnaissance. They strafed and destroyed three Japanese trucks on the Riam road near Cape Lobang, in Borneo. This was typical of the missions flown by the unit in the final months of the war, and it routinely endured losses to the often deadly Japanese flak.

That Flt Lt George Scrimgeour was credited with a half-share in the destruction of No 457 Sqn's final victory was appropriate, for he had enjoyed a lengthy combat career that started with Buffaloes in Malaya in December 1941 (*via J W Bennett*)

The tropical background to No 452 Sqn's dispersal at Balikpapan in July 1945 belies the harsh conditions the units of No 80 Fighter Wing endured in the campaign in the East Indies (R C B Ashworth)

The Australian landings at Balik-papan, in northeastern Borneo, began on 1 July, supported by the Spitfire units. Proving just how deadly the flak was on these sorties, No 452 Sqn lost an aircraft during a raid on Tawao on 10 July. Two days later, Flt Lt Cullen, who was also from this unit, perished when he crashed into the sea off the coast of Borneo after being hit by ground fire whilst attacking a bridge.

Spitfire VIII A58-505/UP-S of No 79 Sqn at Biak in mid-1945, when the unit was engaged in flying hazardous ground attack sorties over the Halmaheras (*via A Price*)

On 13 July a detachment of No 452 Sqn Spitfires became the first aircraft to operate from the new 3000-ft runway at Sepingang, in Balikpapan, which had been created expressly so that RAAF air power could support the land campaign. The unit arrived in company with a US Navy Catalina. Flying from here, the Spitfires strafed dug-in enemy positions on a near-daily basis. Four days after arriving at Sepingang, No 452 Sqn flew a series of close support sorties around Balikpapan, during which time its pilots sank 11 barges. On the 22nd, more sweeps netted the unit four enemy trucks destroyed.

Meanwhile, from Morotai, No 79 Sqn had flown 290 sorties over Halmahera in June alone, targeting a variety of small craft used by the Japanese. For all three RAAF Spitfire units still fighting in this forgotten theatre, the war remained hard and bitter against an uncompromising and fanatical foe.

THE LAST HOORAH

In spite of Australian air superiority, the limited enemy air assets remained active. On the night of 24 July, the Japanese launched their largest air attack since the start of the campaign in Borneo. When an RAAF radar unit detected one raid, a pair of Spitfires was scrambled. In spite of the darkness, Flg Off J C King of No 452 Sqn (in A58-430/QY-V) destroyed one of the intruders before having to break off and return to base short on fuel. Flt Lt Colyer failed to make contact, however. The RAAF's final Spitfire victory was described by the unit's diarist thus;

'To Flg Off King fell the fortune of being the first No 452 Sqn pilot to make contact with the enemy in the air since 24 December last. During the early hours of the morning, indications of a maximum of ten enemy aircraft were plotted by fighter sector, and Flg Off King made contact on two occasions. His first attack was unsuccessful and the contact was lost, but full advantage was taken of the second opportunity, and the squadron score moved along when one, probably a "Helen", went into the sea in flames. King took off at 0220 hrs and landed at 0425 hrs. Nicknamed "Argus", he was regarded as probably the most inoffensive member of the squadron, and was so excited when he returned that he was almost incoherent for half-an-hour afterwards!'

King's significant solitary victory over what was indeed a twin-engined Ki-49 'Helen' was not only the last RAAF air combat victory of the conflict, but also the last of a countless number made by the Spitfire during World War 2. It was not, however, the last Japanese aircraft destroyed, for on 30 and 31 July Spitfires of No 79 Sqn strafed enemy bombers found on the ground at Lolobata airstrip.

Just prior to these sorties, Sarraminde town was attacked for the first time by Spitfires of No 452 Sqn on the 28th, with motor transport and barges being targeted. Flg Off Pretty, who had claimed his only victory on Christmas Eve and was described by his CO as 'a keen and aggressive pilot', led the three aircraft, and he was lucky not to have been shot down by flak.

Flt Lt Scrimgeour's mount when he achieved his victory on 20 June 1945 was A58-631/ZP-V, which is seen here at Tadji during No 457 Sqn's transit home to Australia (*Mackenzie*)

No 79 Sqn also continued attacks on Halmahera until operations were suspended on 14 August. Sadly, 12 days earlier, Flt Lt Barney Newman, who was a veteran of action from the UK in 1941 when he had made several claims, became the squadron's last combat casualty when he was shot down and killed (in A58-654) during a strike against a radio station in the Wasile Bay area of Halmahera.

No 452 Sqn's final sorties of the war were flown on 10 August 1945 when Sqn Ldr Barclay led strafing passes along the Milford Highway, where the unit destroyed a truck, and on enemy positions on the Kahala River. On the 13th (the day before operations were suspended), No 457 Sqn flew the final operational RAAF Spitfire sorties when four aircraft, led by Flt Lt Bell, undertook an armed reconnaissance of the Jesselton area. Later that same day Flt Lt Campbell led another armed reconnaissance flight to the Keningau area. Finally, in the late afternoon, Flt Lt Jenkins and Flt Sgt Gillies were scrambled to search for a Mosquito in distress. They spotted the wreckage to the south of Labuan and, fortunately, the crew were subsequently rescued. It was an appropriately happy ending to the Spitfire's career in the Far East.

Some 16 aces had claimed five or more victories, or increased their existing scores, whilst flying Spitfires in the humid skies of the Southwest Pacific and Burma. It is therefore appropriate that the last word on the classic fighter in combat with the Japanese should belong to one of them, namely Flt Lt Bob Foster;

'In the Far East and Pacific areas, as in any other theatre of war, the Spitfire lived up to its reputation as a formidable fighter aircraft. The Mk VC, with its universal wing that enabled it to carry two 20 mm cannon as well as four machine guns, was able to inflict great, and often fatal, damage to the lightly armoured and relatively slow Japanese bombers. Its speed also overcame the problem associated with the "Dinah", as this high level, fast reconnaissance aircraft had been able to outrun its pursuers until the arrival of the Spitfire – as the Japanese found to their cost over Darwin.

'In spite of problems with serviceability, the aircraft (BR539 DL-X) I flew up from Sydney on 16 January 1943 was still going strong when I last flew it on 28 October, by which time it had clocked up 100+ hours in all weather conditions. In short, the "Spit" didn't let us down in Australia!'

APPENDICES

Spitfire Aces of Burma and the Pacific

Name	Service	Unit/s	Theatre Claims	Total Claims	Area
Caldwell C R	RAAF	1 Wg, 80 Wg 2 OTU	7/3/-	26+4sh/11/25	A
Cross R W	RAF	136	6/-/3	9/1/9	B
Day R W R	RCAF	81, 67	5+1sh/-/1	5+1sh/-/1	B
Gibbs E M	RAF	54	5+1sh/-/5	5+1sh/-/5	A
Foster R W	RAF	54	5/2/2	6+1sh/3/6+1sh	A
Smithson J H*	RAAF	457	5?/-/1	5?/-/3	A
Hall E S*	RAAF	452	3+2sh?/1/2	3+2sh?/1/2	A

Aces with some Spitfire Claims in Burma and the Pacific

Name	Service	Unit/s	Theatre Claims	Total Claims	Area
Goold W A	RAAF	607	4/1/5	5/1/5	B
Conway A G	RAF	136, 155	4/1/3	7/1/4	B
Goldsmith A P	RAAF	452, 2 OTU	4/-/1	16+1sh/2/7	A
Rathwell D W	RAF	81, 17	2+2sh/-/3 or 2/-/3?	3+2sh/1sh/3	B
Constantine A N*	RAF	273, 136	3/3/2	3/3/2	B
Peart A M	RAF	81	3/-/4	6+1sh/-/9	B
Whitamore M M	RAF	81	3/-/3	10+1sh/3+1sh/11	B
Yates J N	RAF	607	2/1/1	4+1sh/2/2	B
Cronin L F M	RAAF	81	2/-/2	5/-/5	B
Smith L A	RAF	152	1/-/1	5+1sh/-/2	B
Lacey J H	RAF	155, 17	1/-/-	28/5/9	B
Bisley J H E	RAAF	452	1/-/-	6+1sh/1/-	A
Collingwood R J P	SAAF	81	1/-/-	5/1/1	B
Holland R H	RAF	615	-/-/1	5+1sh/4/6+1sh	B

Aces who flew Spitfires in Burma and the Pacific but made no Claims

Name	Service	Unit/s	Total Claims	Area
Andrews J R	RAF	607	6/-/4	B
Arthur W S	RAAF	73 Wg, 2 OTU	8/2/6	A
Bocock E P W	RAF	549	5/2/8	A
Boyd R F	RAF	166 Wg, 293 Wg	14+7sh/3/7	B
Brennan V P	RAAF	79 RAAF	10/1/6	A
Carey F H	RAF	AFTU	25+3sh/3/8	B
Charney K L	RAF	132	6/4/7	B
Cock J R	RAF	54, 79 RAAF	10+1sh/4/5	A
Cox D G S R	RAF	909 Wg	7+1sh/6/5	B
Cundy R W	RAAF	452	5+2sh/1/1	A
Elsdon T A F	RAF	165 Wg	7/-/2	B
Finlay D O	RAF	906 Wg	4+2sh/3+1sh/-	B
Forbes A S	RAF	165 Wg	7+2sh/1/-	B
Gibbes R H M	RAAF	2 OTU, 80 Wg	10+2sh/5/16	A
Glendinning A*	RAAF	457, 8 OTU	3+2sh/2/2	A
Ingram M R B	RAF	152	8+6sh/3/5	B
Jeffrey P	RAAF	1 Wg, 2 OTU	5+1sh/-/1	A
Jones N G	RAF	152	6+1sh/-/-	B
Linnard S	RAF	54	6+1sh/3/5	A
Mailey W H A	RAAF	2 OTU	6/-/5	A
Parker T C	RAF	67	2+4sh/-/3	B
Parkinson C H	RAAF	457	8+1sh/3+1sh/7	A
Pegge C O J	RAF	607	8/2/8	B
Rawlinson A C	RAAF	79 RAAF, 73 Wg	8/2/8	A
Reid L S*	RAAF	79 RAAF, 452, 2 OTU	4/1/6	A
Sanderson J G	RAAF	452	3+2sh/2/1	A
Smith D H	RAAF	452	5+1sh/2/2	A
Smith F V*	RAF	902 Wg	2+1sh/1/1	B
Steege G H	RAAF	73 Wg	8/2/5	A
Stephen H M	RAF	166 Wg	9+8sh/3/7	B
Storey W J	RAAF	CGS	8/2/-	A
Sutton F B	RAF	293 Wg	4+1sh/2/1	B
Thorold-Smith R E	RAAF	452	6+sh/-/1	A
Thorpe A S	RAF	165 Wg	7+2sh/1/-	B
Vanderfield D	RAAF	79 RAAF	5/1sh/-	A
Waddy J L	RAAF	2 OTU	15+1sh/7/6	A
Wilkinson R C	RAF	1 Wg	7+3sh/-/1	A
Williams G A *	RAF	67	3+1sh/2/4	B

Non-Ace Pilots with five or more Spitfire Claims in Burma and the Pacific

Name	Service	Unit/s	Area Claims	Total Claims	Area
Butler V B G	RAF	136	2/2/1	2+1sh/2/1	B
Gannon K F	RAAF	615	2/1/3	2/1/3	B
Garvan D E W	RAAF	136	4/2/4	4/2/4	B
James W D	RAF	607	2/-/5	2/1sh/8	B
Krohn I R	RAF	81, 155	1/1/7	2+1sh/2/8	B
Lee P H	RAF	165 Wg, 170 Wg	3/1/2	3/1/2	B
MacLean D H	RAAF	457	1+2sh/-/3	1+2sh/2/4+1sh	A
Moorhouse G J	RAF	136	2/-/3	2/-/4	B
Watson P H	RAAF	457	4/-/2	4/-/3	A
Watson R W	RAAF	457, 452	2+1sh/-/3	2+1sh/-/3	A

Non-Ace Spitfire Pilots in Burma and the Pacific with five or more Claims in total

Name	Service	Unit/s	Area Claims	Total Claims	Area
Andrews G W	RAAF	615	2/1/1	3/1/4	B
Bargh C V	RNZAF	67	3/2/-	3/2/-	B
Boardman L L	RAAF	457, 85	2/2/2	2/2/2	A
Briggs J L	RAF	607	-/-/3	2/-/3	B
Brown E	RAF	136	2/1/1	4/1/1	B
Bunting K	RAF	136	1/-/1	2/-/3	B
Carroll A G	RAF	615	2/-/1	2/-/3	B
Chandler H A	RNZAF	615	3/-/1	3/-/3	B
Doudy C T	RAAF	607, 136	1/1/2	2/1/3	B
Glaser E D	RAF	549, 548	3sh/1/-	3sh/1/-	A
James K E*	RAAF	457, 85 RAAF, 79 RAAF	2?/1/-	2?/1/-	A
Jones M S	RAF	152	-/-/1	2/1/3	B
Laundy S C J	RAF	54	2/1/1	2/1/1	A
Louis P G	RAF	615	2sh/-/-	1+2sh/1/-	B
MacDonald R S	RAAF	452	2/-/-	2/-/-	A
Mower G A	RAAF	54, 452	3/-/1	3/-/2	A
Robinson W J	RNZAF	81	-/1/2	2/1/3	B
Rudling J D	RNZAF	136	1/-/3	2/-/5	B
Simpson C M	RNZAF	67	2/-/-	2/-/-	B
Trimble T H	RAAF	457	2/-/5	2/-/5	A
Weggery S L E	RNZAF	615	2sh/-/2	2sh/-/2	B
Wilding F E	RAF	136	2/-/2	4/2/2	B

Notes

Those pilots with less than five victories or claims are marked thus * and are shown because of their inclusion in *Aces High* or *Those Other Eagles* where there may be doubt as to their actual scores

Theatre Abbreviations

B - Burma and India

A - Australia and the Southwest Pacific

1

Spitfire VC BS295/CR-C of Wg Cdr C R Caldwell, No 1 Fighter Wing, Strauss, Northern Territory, March 1943

Having been appointed as the CO of No 1 Fighter Wing in Darwin, Clive Caldwell kept his RAF practice by identifying his personal aircraft with his initials. He had several assigned Spitfires, one of which was BS295, which he flew in his first combat with the Japanese on 2 March 1943 when he was credited with two kills. Seeing further action on 20 and 30 June, he was credited with two more Zero-sens destroyed and two 'Bettys' as probables – the majority of his seven confirmed against the Japanese came in BS295. It wore the standard RAAF camouflage, with the addition of a striped spinner. After Caldwell BS295 served with both Nos 452 and 457 Sqns.

2

Spitfire VC BS231/D of Sqn Ldr R E Thorold-Smith, No 452 Sqn RAAF, Strauss, Northern Territory, March 1943

Twenty-two-year-old Australian 'Throttle' Thorold-Smith served in the UK with No 452 Sqn, with whom he gained 6.5 victories, before accompanying the unit back to his homeland, having succeeded 'Bluey' Truscott as CO. On 15 March 1943, when at the controls of BS231 (which did not have unit codes), he led a scramble of Spitfires from No 1 Fighter Wing against an incoming raid of around 25 Japanese bombers. The latter were sighted west of Point Charles, and Thorold-Smith led his section in on them. The RAAF fighters were immediately attacked from three sides by the escorting Zero-sens, and Thorold-Smith was shot down and killed. Many years later, parts of his aircraft were recovered and are now on display in the museum of the Aviation Society of the Northern Territory in Darwin.

3

Spitfire VC BR539/DL-X of Flt Lt R W Foster, No 54 Sqn, Winnellie, Northern Territory, March-July 1943

This aircraft was the regular mount of Flt Lt Bob Foster, who, in February 1943, had claimed the first Spitfire victory over the Japanese, although in another fighter. He was, however, at the controls of BS539 on 15 March when he brought down a 'Betty' and claimed another as a probable whilst defending Darwin. Foster used it again during his next successful combat on 20 June, when he destroyed a Zero-sen to achieve 'acedom'. In his final combat on 6 July, Foster downed a 'Betty' and claimed a second as a probable, again in BR539. These kills meant that he was one of just a handful of pilots to have achieved five victories in Spitfires against the Japanese. Foster was awarded a DFC soon afterwards, while BR539 was later transferred to a training unit and written off in 1945.

4

Spitfire VC BS186/QY-L of Flt Lt E S Hall, No 452 Sqn RAAF, Strauss, Northern Territory, March-June 1943

'Smithy' Hall originally served in the UK with No 129 Sqn, before returning to Australia as a flight commander with No 452 Sqn. With the latter unit he was allocated this aircraft, which he flew throughout his tour. Initially, it did not wear unit codes but did carry the inscription *D.M.L. OVERDALE* forward of the cockpit – unit codes were later applied as are shown

here. Hall made four claims against the Japanese (all Zero-sens), of which two were destroyed. His known claims are for 2.5 destroyed, one probable and two damaged, although his total destroyed may in fact be three, with two shared. BS186 ended its service career as a ground instructional airframe.

5

Spitfire VC BS164/DL-K of Sqn Ldr E M Gibbs, No 54 Sqn, Winnellie, Northern Territory, May 1943

Thirty-year-old former Halton apprentice Eric Gibbs led No 54 Sqn to Australia, where, in action against the Japanese between March and July 1943, he made 11 claims during the raids on Darwin, including 5.5 destroyed – all of them while flying this aircraft. During the first raid intercepted by Spitfires on 2 March Gibbs claimed a Zero-sen destroyed. His most successful action was on 30 June when, during a sortie filled with intensive combat which took him to 'acedom', he was credited with a 'Betty' and a Zero-sen destroyed, as well as a half-share in the destruction of a second bomber and the damaging of two more G4Ms. After a very successful tour, Gibbs left No 54 Sqn in January 1944. That same month BS164 was destroyed in a collision near Strauss, killing the pilot – ironically, a Flt Sgt Gibbs. It is shown here following Gibbs' second kill on 2 May.

6

Spitfire VC BS305/DL-J of Flt Lt J R Cock, No 54 Sqn, Winnellie, Northern Territory, 1 June 1943

South Australian John Cock had joined the RAF just before World War 2, and emerged from the fighting in France and the Battle of Britain as an ace with 10.5 victories. After a period instructing and further service in the UK, he was posted to Australia, where he joined No 54 Sqn near Darwin in mid-1943. He flew BS305 for the first time on 1 June during a wing practice scramble, the flight lasting just over an hour. Cock later returned to the UK, where he flew Tempests with No 3 Sqn. During September, BS305 was flown by fellow Australian ace Wg Cdr Peter Jeffrey in a series of practice scrambles.

7

Spitfire VC JG740/UP-U of Sqn Ldr A C Rawlinson, No 79 Sqn RAAF, Vivigangi and Kiriwina, New Guinea, June-November 1943

The first CO of the first Spitfires deployed to New Guinea was Sqn Ldr Alan Rawlinson, who was an eight-victory ace from the desert fighting. After No 79 Sqn formed in Australia, he led his new unit into action against the Japanese, but there were few contacts with the JAAF. Lacking a Vokes filter, JG740 was Rawlinson's regular mount, and he named it *Sweet FA* – his No 3 Sqn RAAF Tomahawk had also featured this nickname. This Spitfire was also flown on occasion by other aces, including Flt Lt Doug Vanderfield and Wg Cdr 'Woof' Arthur. JG740 later transferred to the CGS, but it was wrecked after it suffered and in-flight engine failure on 21 December 1944.

8

Spitfire VC JK225/ZP-L of Flg Off J H Smithson, No 452 Sqn RAAF, Strauss, Northern Territory, September 1943

Although Victorian John Smithson appears to have been credited with four victories, the citation for his DFC (awarded for the outstanding feat of destroying two 'Bettys' over Darwin at night on 12 November 1943) stated that he had five destroyed, as did a report by his CO, which also listed some additional probable and damaged claims. Either way, Smithson was a very successful pilot who regularly flew JK225 during his tour. Indeed, he used it on 7 September when, at 25,000 ft over the Middle Arm, near Darwin, he downed a Zero-sen. JK225 was wrecked in a landing accident at Livingstone on 19 October.

9
Spitfire VC LZ862 of Flt Lt J L Waddy, No 2 OTU, Mildura, Victoria, September 1943-February 1944

This aircraft was delivered to No 2 OTU on 13 September 1943, where it was used to convert new pilots to the Spitfire and prepare them for action against the Japanese. One of the instructors with the unit was Flt Lt John Waddy, who had claimed 15.5 kills during his service in the Middle East in 1942-43. He regularly flew LZ862, which carried its number in chrome yellow on the fuselage, until it caught fire and crashed on 23 February 1944.

10
Spitfire VC MA383 of Sqn Ldr A N Constantine, No 136 Sqn, Baigachi, India, 10 October 1943

MA383 (thought to later have been coded 'HM-A') was the first Spitfire VC to be delivered to No 136 Sqn at Baigachi, near Calcutta, in early October 1943. It was initially flown by the unit on 10 October, when the unit's CO, Sqn Ldr Noel Constantine, flew circuits in it for 20 minutes. He noted, 'Lovely machine, light, graceful, fast – oh, so much faster than the beloved "Hurribuses"!' Constantine, who had flown Defiants during the Battle of Britain, had all his success with Spitfire VCs over Burma, totalling at least eight claims. MA383 later joined No 615 Sqn and crashed near Palel during an interception on 29 May 1944, killing the pilot, Sgt H K Young.

11
Spitfire VC JG807/UP-P of Flt Lt R D Vanderfield, No 79 Sqn RAAF, Vivigangi and Kiriwina, New Guinea, July-December 1943

Until RAAF serials were introduced in late November 1943, A58-176 carried the RAF serial JG807. It was regularly flown by Flt Lt Doug Vanderfield, who had become an ace whilst flying Buffalos over Malaya, throughout his period with No 79 Sqn, the first time being on a scramble from Vivigangi on 8 July. It was also flown by Sgt I H Callister, when he shot down a Ki-61 'Tony' 40 miles north of Kiriwina on 31 October. As well as its camouflage, the aircraft wears the white tail and wing leading edge markings introduced in the SWPA as an identity feature. It was later transferred to No 85 Sqn and sold for scrap in 1948.

12
Spitfire VC A58-254/QY-F of Flt Lt A P Goldsmith, No 452 Sqn RAAF, Strauss, Northern Territory, 10 January 1944

Adrian Goldsmith had been credited with 16.5 victories during his service in Malta and Darwin, and he was one of only a handful of aces to include German, Italian and Japanese aircraft in his score. By the time he flew A58-254 (previously MH591), Japanese raids had ceased, but standby was maintained. On 10 January 1944, Goldsmith was scrambled in this aircraft in

company with three pilots, including fellow ace Flt Lt Ron Cundy, after an unknown 'plot' that turned out to be a friendly B-25. He later served as an instructor, and this aircraft was also used for training at the CGS until it belly-landed on 18 April 1945 and was declared a write-off.

13
Spitfire VC A58-220/QY-R of Flg Off J H E Bisley, No 452 Sqn RAAF, Strauss, Northern Territory, 13 January 1944

Having achieved ace status during his service in Malta, John Bisley joined No 452 Sqn when it was re-established in Australia. He saw considerable service with the unit and scrambled many times against Japanese aircraft. During the 20 June 1943 raid, he claimed a 'Betty' destroyed ten miles off Cape Gambier, although Bisley had in fact downed a Ki-49 heavy bomber – his final victory, and his only success over the Japanese. Bisley left the unit for instructional duties and flew A58-220 on what may have been his final scramble, which, in the event proved to be uneventful. A59-220 remained with No 452 Sqn until it suffered a wheels-up landing on 31 May 1944.

14
Spitfire VC MH300/KW-S of Flg Off P G Louis, No 615 'County of Surrey' Sqn, Dohazari, India, 16 January 1944

Flg Off Paul Louis had been credited with a half-share in the first Spitfire kill over Burma in November 1943, and he first flew MH300 on Christmas Day 1943, soon after it had been delivered. Over the next few days he scrambled several times in it, but with no contact. On 16 January he scrambled in MH300 from Dohazari with Flg Off Weggery after a Ki-46, and in a five-minute combat they succeeded in shooting it down. Louis left No 615 Sqn soon afterwards, although MH300 remained, being flown by other notable pilots including Flt Lt Kevin Gannon and Plt Off 'Nappy' Carroll. It was written off when a tyre burst on take-off on 12 April.

15
Spitfire VC MA292/KW-D of Flg Off S L E Weggery, No 615 'County of Surrey' Sqn, Dohazari, India, 16 January and 26 April 1944

Both the victories claimed by New Zealander Lawrence Weggery were shared with Paul Louis, and on the second of these he was flying this aircraft. Both pilots had suffered gun jamming problems during the interception, thus presenting them with some real difficulties when it came to aiming! MA292 was named VERNA JUNE II, and as well as featuring a New Zealand fern leaf on the nose, it was also decorated with two victory symbols. Weggery saw further combat with MA292 on 26 April south of Imphal, when he damaged two Ki-43s. The aircraft did not survive much longer, however, for it was force-landed in a paddy field on 24 May.

16
Spitfire VIII JG183/RD-S of Flg Off C V Bargh, No 67 Sqn, Alipore, India, 29 February 1944

JG183 had a long career with No 67 Sqn, beginning in late February 1944 when the newly re-equipped unit had its first scramble when 'Pink' and 'Brown' Sections were launched, although it was abortive. On that occasion it was flown by a successful New Zealand pilot Flg Off 'Ketchil' Bargh, who had already had five claims, including three destroyed, to his credit.

JG183 served with the veteran squadron for much of 1944, and on New Year's Day 1945 it was flown by another successful pilot in the form of Flt Lt Clyde Simpson. Its long career finally came to an end on 1 March when a hung up bomb came off when it was landing at Dabaing.

17
Spitfire VIII JF698/FL-J of Sqn Ldr W M Whitamore, No 81 Sqn, 'Broadway' strip, Burma, 13 March 1944
Twenty-one year old 'Babe' Whitamore led No 81 Sqn out to the Burma theatre, where JF698 – which bore the unit's famous 'Ace of Spades' marking – became his regular mount. He claimed his first victory against the Japanese flying it on 13 February 1944, when he shot down a Ki-43 off the Mayu peninsula of the Arakan. Exactly a month later, Whitamore was at its controls again when he led a detachment from Imphal forward to the Chindit base at 'Broadway', from where he shot down another 'Oscar' to claim his squadron's 100th victory. On 17 March, when flying another aircraft, Whitamore was killed in a gallant attempt to defend 'Broadway' from an enemy attack. JF698 was subsequently flown on occasions by other No 81 Sqn aces Flg Off Alan Peart and Capt R J P Collingwood.

18
Spitfire VIII JF835/UM-T of Sqn Ldr M R B Ingram, No 152 Sqn, Chittagong, India, 6 April 1944
New Zealand-born 14-victory ace Bruce Ingram was an inspirational leader of his squadron, which he had commanded since the Sicilian campaign, prior to bringing it to India. Once in the Far East, his unit was initially employed in the defence of Calcutta so there was little chance to engage the Japanese. This particular aircraft was the regular mount of Ingram's deputy, Capt W J Hoffe of the SAAF. However, on 6 April Ingram flew it when he led an escort for a VIP flight transporting the Viceroy of India, Viscount Wavell, to the front. Two months later Ingram was injured in an accident, and he contracted a disease from which he sadly died. JF835 wears the original form of No 152 Sqn's Black Panther marking, which was soon applied over the roundels.

19
Spitfire VIII MT567/HM-B of Flt Sgt R W Cross, No 136 Sqn, Wanjing, India, 6 April 1944
With nine victories to his name, Bob Cross was the top scoring Commonwealth pilot in the Burma theatre. Six of his successes came while flying the Spitfire, and he was in fact the second most successful Spitfire pilot against the Japanese. Cross is not thought to have engaged in any combats when flying this aircraft, but on 6 April 1944 he flew it on an uneventful dawn patrol over the Imphal area. MT567 was later transferred to No 67 Sqn, and it survived the war to become an exhibition airframe.

20
Spitfire VIII JG560 of Wg Cdr F R Carey, AFTU, Armada Road, India, April-November 1944
Frank Carey was one of the outstanding fighter leaders of World War 2, and he ended up with 28 victories – all claimed on Hurricanes. In 1943 he formed the Air Fighting Training Unit (AFTU) in India to provide tactical and air gunnery training to Allied fighter pilots. The unit flew a variety of types, and after its introduction to service in India, a number of Spitfires were also supplied to the AFTU. Carey adopted JG560 as his personal mount, and he had it adorned with a red spinner and striking red and white fuselage flash so that his pupils would recognise him when they flew mock combats!

21
Spitfire VIII A58-435/QY-T of Flt Lt W R Cundy, No 452 Sqn RAAF, Sattler, Northern Territory, July-September 1944
By the time he joined No 452 Sqn in his homeland, Australia, in 1943, 21-year-old Ron Cundy was a much decorated desert ace. Initially serving as an instructor, he returned to operations in October 1943 as a flight commander with No 452 Sqn. Although he was scrambled several times against the last Japanese incursions, he failed to add to his victory tally. In mid-1944 Cundy was allocated Spitfire VIII A58-435 as his personal aircraft, and he had it adorned with a personal 'pegasus' motif. The fighter is thought to have been camouflaged in just foliage green and sky blue, and it was kept well polished by his groundcrew. When Cundy eventually transferred out of the unit, he left A58-435 behind with considerable regret. The fighter was lost in a collision with a B-24D during a fighter affiliation exercise near Melville Island on 18 September 1944.

22
Spitfire VIII A58-354/DL-V of Sqn Ldr S Linnard, No 54 Sqn, Livingstone, Northern Territory, August-September 1944
Sid Linnard had achieved 'acedom' over Greece and the desert during 1940-41, and he assumed command of No 54 Sqn in mid-1944, by which time Darwin was an operational backwater. Nonetheless, he did participate in some of the few operational ground attack sorties flown by his unit. During the early part of his tenure as CO, Linnard flew A58-354, and, as was usual for No 54 Sqn Spitfires, the individual aircraft letter was applied in white. Linnard eventually returned to the UK, whilst this aircraft also survived to be scrapped post-war.

23
Spitfire VC A58-104 of Sqn Ldr W J Storey, CGS, Cressy, Victoria, September 1944-September 1945
A schoolmaster from Victoria, Jack Storey was the most successful Hurricane pilot against the Japanese, his eight kills also making him the leading RAAF pilot against them too. After his service in Burma he returned to Australia on promotion in 1944, where he became CO of the Central Gunnery School and put his expertise to good use. There, Storey regularly flew this Mk VC that had previously seen action with No 79 Sqn. Indeed, Flg Off Jim Richards had been flying it when he shared in the destruction of a Ki-61 near Kiriwina on 21 December 1943 to help claim No 79 Sqn's final air combat victory.

24
Spitfire VIII A58-379/ZF-Z of Sqn Ldr E P W Bocock, No 549 Sqn, Strauss, Northern Territory, 1 October 1944
A58-379 was the regular aircraft of Flt Lt Dave Glaser, who had gained three shared victories and a probable in 1940-42 prior to joining No 549 Sqn in Australia. There, he saw little action, although on 21 August 1944 he scrambled in it to identify an unidentified aircraft, but this proved to be friendly. No 549 Sqn's CO was five-victory ace Sqn Ldr Eric Bocock, who, on 1 October flew this aircraft on an air-to-ground firing sortie. The previous month, on 5 September, Glaser had flown A58-379

during a strafing attack, led by Bocock, on Selaroe Island – one of the squadron's few combat missions. Interestingly, it wore a colourful 'musketeer' marking on its natural metal finish.

25
Spitfire VC A58-252/UP-A of Flt Lt L S Reid, No 79 Sqn RAAF, Momote, New Guinea, 4 October 1944
This was the regular aircraft of No 79 Sqn's CO, Sqn Ldr Stan Galton, and it carried the name *JEN*[III] on both sides of the fuse-lage. It had a short life with the unit, having been delivered on 7 August 1944 and written off in a landing accident on 4 October, when flown by Flt Lt Len Reid (who had achieved much success flying Spitfires over Malta). As he took off on a local practice flight, the aircraft blew a tyre on the rough strip causing Reid to swing off into a ditch and turn over. He was uninjured, but when the aircraft was righted, its back was broken. Although thought to be wearing normal camouflage, it is possible that A58-252 was painted in Foliage Green and Sky Blue, as it had been at No 1 Aircraft Depot at the same time as the RAAF's first Spitfire VIIIs were being painted in this scheme.

26
Spitfire VIII LV678/DG-C of Flg Off A H Witteridge, No 155 Sqn, Palel, India, September-November 1944
In September 1944, 'Witt' Witteridge was allocated LV678/DG-C as his own aircraft, which his groundcrew decorated with the Chindit badge in honour of their XIVth Army colleagues. They also made some modifications to the fighter, including removing the rear view mirror, outboard machine guns, ballast in the tail, armour plate behind the pilot's seat and the emergency canopy lock. They also polished the wing leading edges, prompting Witteridge to comment that it was 'Quite a boy racer'! It certainly made its mark on the enemy, as on 25 September Witterige intercepted and destroyed a high flying Ki-46. Then, on 7 October, Flg Off 'Babe' Hunter was flying LV678 when he shot down another 'Dinah', while on 5 November Witteridge destroyed a Ki-43 'Oscar'.

27
Spitfire VIII A58-514/ZP-Q of Flt Lt A Glendinning, No 457 Sqn RAAF, Sattler, Northern Territory, late 1944
Flt Lt Alf Glendinning may have scored as many as five victories (two of them shared) over the desert in 1942-43, before returning to his native Australia in early 1944, where he joined No 457 Sqn. Toward the end of his tour he flew A58-514 on routine and monotonous defensive operations from the Darwin area. As well as wearing two-tone green camouflage, this aircraft also carried a red spinner. Glendinning finished his tour at the end of the year and returned to duty as an instructor, while his mount also survived the war.

28
Spitfire VIII MD215/DG-Y of Sqn Ldr J H Lacey, No 155 Sqn, Palel, India, 7-8 November 1944
One of the RAF's leading aces of the war, 'Ginger' Lacey had served in India as an air gunnery instructor under Wg Cdr Frank Carey. In later 1944 he returned to operations, but before assuming command of No 17 Sqn, he was attached for a few weeks to No 155 Sqn. On 7 November Lacey flew the first sortie with the unit in this aircraft when, shortly before 1600 hrs, he took off for a one hour 'sector recce'. The following after-

noon he was again at its controls when he led a patrol of the Tiddim-Kaleymo-Maulaik areas, during which he spotted some radial-engined aircraft. Lacey chased them as far as Khumbirigram, where they were identified as P-47s. Although uneventful, this was the 27-kill ace's first Spitfire operation.

29
Spitfire VIII A58-528/CRC of Wg Cdr C R Caldwell, No 80 Fighter Wing, Morotai, Netherlands East Indies, January-March 1945
A58-528 was one of several aircraft that Caldwell was allocated during his time as CO of No 80 Fighter Wing. Available evidence suggests that it had overall Foliage Green uppersurfaces and, unlike his other mounts, his initials were positioned aft of the roundels and not bisected by them. By this time there were few Japanese aircraft left in the area, so Caldwell led his wing on ground strafing work. His last war operations were flown in this aircraft – on 25 March 1945 he flew it from Manila to Bataan and Corregidor, while his very last wartime flight was a recce to Tarakan on the 28th. A58-528 crashed at Clark Field, Manila, whilst being flown by Flt Lt Ted Sly on 3 May.

30
Spitfire VIII JG567/RD-A of Sqn Ldr R W R Day, No 67 Sqn, Maunghnama, Burma, 9 January 1945
Flying ex-No 607 Sqn aircraft JG567, which wore the name *Mary Anne*, No 67's recently appointed CO Sqn Ldr Bob Day led a section of five Spitfires that were scrambled against a Japanese air attack on shipping around Akyab on 9 January 1945. The enemy formation was comprised of Ki-43s and Ki-84s. Climbing rapidly above the escorts, Day spotted the six Ki-43s led by 64th Sentai CO, Maj Toyoki Eto, and he immediately dived on them. In a brief fight, five were claimed shot down, including two to Bob Day. His final victories took him to 'acedom', all of which were claimed whilst flying Spitfires in Burma. All of Eto's wingmen were killed, while Eto himself had to crash-land his damaged fighter at Myebon. Day received a DFC soon afterwards, but he was then involved in a road accident that ruled him out of further operational flying.

31
Spitfire VIII A58-602/RG-V of Wg Cdr R H M Gibbes, No 80 Fighter Wing, Tarakan, Borneo, January-April 1945
After distinguished service in the Middle East, where he had gained a dozen victories, Gibbes joined No 80 Fighter WIng in the Southwest Pacific as Wing Leader. The wing concentrated on ground attack work, as by this time there was little in the way of enemy air activity. In January 1945 Gibbes adopted A58-602 as his personal aircraft. As was his privilege, it carried his initials (RG), while the 'V' recalled the usual letter worn by his various P-40s in the desert. Unusually, the fighter is painted in the standard RAF temperate colour scheme, and it also carries *Grey Nurse* titling and the sharksmouth marking that adorned the Spitfires of No 457 Sqn. The fighter also boasts Gibbes' not inconsiderable 'scoreboard'.

32
Spitfire VIII MT879/UM-F of Flg Off L A Smith, No 152 Sqn, Sinthe, Burma, March 1945
On 2 March 1945 Flg Off Len Smith, who had 5.5 victories (including one against the JAAF) flew an uneventful patrol at the

controls of MT879. This sortie was led by WO Duval, who, with Smith, was responsible for the decoration of No 152 Sqn's Spitfires with the distinctive 'leaping panther' marking that surrounded the roundels. Smith was flying MT879 again on the 26th when he participated in a strafing mission against Japanese positions south of Letse. The aircraft was also regularly flown by No 152 Sqn's CO, Sqn Ldr Grant Kerr, and it was struck off charge at the end of the war.

33

Spitfire VIII JG534/AF-Z of Flg Off J R Andrew, No 607 'County of Durham' Sqn, Mingaladon, Burma, 10 June 1945

Twenty-three-year-old Yorkshireman James Andrew had become an ace over Italy in 1944, and towards the end of the year had joined No 607 Sqn in Burma. Most of the activity undertaken by fighter units in-theatre now consisted of ground attack sorties in support of the Army, as well as escorting vital transport aircraft. It was on one such mission whilst escorting a C-47 drop over Burma on 10 June that Andrew flew JG534 for the first time, and later that day he flew it again on a recon-naissance sortie. However, on the 25th he continued alone on a ground attack sortie over the Sittang River from which the six-victory ace did not return. Andrew was the last Spitfire ace lost in Burma. JG534, however, survived the war and was struck off charge on 14 March 1946.

34

Spitfire VIII MT904/AF-X of Sqn Ldr C O J Pegge, No 607 'County of Durham' Sqn, Mingaladon, Burma, June-July 1945

Pegge was a Battle of Britain ace who took command of No 607 Sqn at the end of June 1945. He occasionally flew MT904 on sorties against the retreating Japanese throughout his brief tenure. One such occasion was 13 July, when he flew it on a bombing and strafing sortie in support of the Army on the Sittang bend. Both Pegge and this aircraft remained with the unit until its disbandment in mid-August. MT904 wears the standard colours for the period, including the white identity markings that were introduced earlier in the year.

35

Spitfire VIII MV483/DG-A of Sqn Ldr A G Conway, No 155 Sqn, Thedaw, Burma, late July 1945

Seven-victory ace Gordon Conway achieved all his successes with No 136 Sqn in the Burma campaign, four of them whilst flying Spitfires. In mid-1945 he was given command of No 155 Sqn, which was then mainly engaged on ground attack work. Conway flew this aircraft, which wore a distinctive quartered diamond marking on the nose, on a number of occasions dur-ing late July. On the 26th he flew it in a bombing and strafing attack on Kyauki, and repeated this the following day against targets in Thaunbo and Myete. Then, on the 28th, he flew it on two more ground attack missions. At the end of the war Conway led his squadron to Singapore, and he was transferred out in November. MV483 was lost soon afterwards in a colli-sion over Arnhemia, Sumatra, on 26 February 1946.

36

Spitfire VC A58-248/SH-Z of Sqn Ldr K E James, No 85 Sqn RAAF, Pearce, Western Australia, July-August 1945

Ken James had originally served in the UK with No 457 Sqn, returning to Australia with them in 1942. There, he regularly engaged Japanese incursions against Darwin and shot down two high-flying Ki-46s. In 1944 James was promoted and given command of No 85 Sqn, which was tasked with the defence of Western Australia. The unit was re-equipped with Spitfire VCs in September 1944, all of which were left unpainted. A58-248, as was appropriate for the CO's aircraft, carried his rank pennant. On 16 August 1945 James suffered an engine failure in this machine and force landed at Parkes. The aircraft was not repaired.

BIBLIOGRAPHY

Air Ministry. *Wings of the Phoenix (The Official History).* HMSO, 1949

Alexander, Kristen, *Clive Caldwell - Air Ace.* Allen & Unwin, 2006

Bowyer, Michael, *Fighting Colours.* PSL, 1969 and 1975

Eather, Steve, *Flying Squadrons of the Australian Defence Force.* Aerospace Publications, 1995

Flintham, Vic & Thomas, Andrew, *Combat Codes.* Airlife, 2003 and 2008

Franks, Norman, *Spitfires over the Arakan.* William Kimber, 1988

Franks, Norman, *The Air Battle for Imphal.* William Kimber, 1985

Franks, Norman, *Frank 'Chota' Carey.* Grub St, 2006

Halley, James, *Squadrons of the RAF & Commonwealth.* Air Britain, 1988

Herrington, John, *Australians in the War 1939-45, Series 3 Volume 3.* Halstead Press, 1962

Hunt, Leslie, *Twenty One Squadrons.* Garnstone Press, 1972

Jefford, Wg Cdr C G, *RAF Squadrons.* Airlife 1988 and 2001

Milberry, Larry & Halliday, Hugh, *The Royal Canadian Air Force at War 1939-1945.* CANAV Books, 1990

Pentland, Geoffrey, *RAAF Camouflage and Markings, Vols 1 & 2.* Kookaburra, 1977

Rawlings, John D R, *Fighter Squadrons of the RAF.* Macdonald, 1969

Richards, Denis, *RAF Official History 1939-45, Parts 2 & 3.* HMSO, 1954

Robertson, Bruce, *Spitfire - The story of a Famous Fighter.* Harleyford, 1960

Shores, Christopher & Williams, Clive, *Aces High Vol 1.* Grub St, 1994

Shores, Christopher, *Aces High Vol 2.* Grub St, 1999

Shores, Christopher, *Those Other Eagles.* Grub St, 2004

Shores, Christopher, *Air War for Burma.* Grub St, 2005

Sturtivant, Ray et al, *Spitfire International.* Air Britain,

Waters, Gp Capt Gary, *OBOE - Air Operations over Borneo 1945.* APSC, 1995

ACKNOWLEDGEMENTS

The author wishes to record his gratitude to the following former Spitfire pilots who have given of their time in answering queries and presenting accounts of their actions for inclusion within this volume – the late Wg Cdr A G Conway DFC, Sqn Ldr M C C Cotton DFC, the late Gp Capt T A F Elsdon OBE DFC, Wg Cdr R W Foster DFC, the late Sqn Ldr E D Glaser DFC AE, Sqn Ldr V K Jacobs, Sqn Ldr W J Storey DFC and Flt Lt A H Witteridge DFC. The author is also most grateful to the many friends and fellow enthusiasts who have generously given support to bring this volume to fruition.

INDEX

References to illustrations are shown in **bold**. Plates are shown with page and caption locators in (brackets).

'Admin Box' 37
Andrew, Flg Off James R 47, **33**(57, 95), 59, **71**, **72**, 72
Andrews, Flg Off Bill 31, **32**
Appleton, Plt Off W H **7**
Ardeline, Flg Off P 63
Arthur, Wg Cdr W S 'Woof' 73, 74, **75**
Ashby, Flg Off Bob 10, **21**

Bargh, Plt Off C V 'Ketchil' 40, **16**(52, 92–93), **61**
Barnett, Flg Off D J **33**
Barrie, Plt Off Jim 75
Beale, Flg Off 16
Begbie, Flt Lt Don **21**
Berry, Flt Sgt 44
Bisley, Flt Lt John H E **16**, 16–17, 23, 25, **13**(52, 92)
Blake, Flg Off A H 15, 16
Bocock, Sqn Ldr Eric P W **24**(54, 93–94), **80**, 80, 82, 83
Bofors gun **68**
Bott, Sqn Ldr Max 74, 76
Boyd, Wg Cdr Finlay 27, 30
Brennan, Flg Off Vic 73
Brinsley, Flt Lt **76**
British and Commonwealth Army: IV Corps 33–34, 66; XIVth Army 66, 67; XV Indian Corps 37, 40, 66; 2nd Div. 60; 5th Indian Div. 30, 40, 60; 7th Indian Div. 30, 36, 40; 9th Australian Div. 74, 84; 12th Army 70; 19th Indian Div. 67, 69, 71; 20th Div. 68; 23rd Brigade 84; 25th Indian Div. 66; 36th Div. 66; 81st West African Div. 30, 34, 40, 66; Chindits 41, 42, 44, 58, 61, 63, 94
'Broadway' airstrip 41, 42, 43, 44, 93
Brook, Flg Off Tony **21**
Brown, Flt Lt Eric 'Bojo' **30**, 30, 33, 36, 40
Bruce, Flg Off E P 64

Caldwell, Gp Capt Clive R **8**, 8, **9**, 9–10, 11, 13–14, 16, 18, 19, **23**, 23–24, **24**, 25, **1**(49, 91), **29**(56, 94), **77**, 77, 79, 82
Caldwell, Plt Off D 48
Callister, Sqn Ian 74, **75**
Campbell, Sgt A 42
Campbell, Flt Lt J G B **84**, 84–85, 87
Carey, Gp Capt Frank R **20**(53, 93), 60, 60–61
Carroll, Flg Off A G 'Nappy' 29, 47, **60**
Chapple, WO A 62
Chatfield, Flg Off H B 'Bert' 31, **32**, 58, 59
Churchill, Winston 6, 7, 11, 33
Cock, Flt Lt John R **16**, 16, **6**(50, 91), 74
Collingwood, Capt Robert 'Moon' 42, 47
Connell, Flg Off Bob 68, **70**, 70
Constantine, Sqn Ldr A Noel 28, **33**, 33, 35–36, 39–40, **10**(51, 92)
Conway, Sqn Ldr A Gordon 32–33, **33**, 34, 40, **35**(57, 95), 70–71, **71**
Coombes, Flt Lt Mike 46, 47–48
Cooper, Sgt Bert 8, 12
Coulter, Plt Off W J 43, 44
Courtney, Wg Cdr R N N **72**
Cox, Wg Cdr David 70
Crawford, Sgt Derek 70
Cronin, Flg Off Larry 41–42, **42**, 45
Cross, Flt Sgt R W 'Bob' 31–32, **32**, 33, 36, 37–38, **43**, 43, **19**(53, 93)
Cullen, Flt Lt 86
Cundy, Flt Lt W Ron 25, **21**(54, 93), 79, **80**
Curtin, John 11, 14

Darwin 6–7, 8, 9, 11, 13, 17, 18, 26
Davies, Sqn Ldr G G A 47, 48, 58, 59
Day, Sqn Ldr R W R 'Bob' 38, 39, 42, 44, 46, 47, **30**(56, 94), 66, **67**, 67
Doudy, Flg Off Colin **29**, 40
Drake, Wg Cdr R E **67**

Elsdon, Wg Cdr Jimmy **30**, 30, 40
Eto, Maj Toyoki 66, 67, 94

Finlay, Gp Capt Don **68**
Foster, Flt Lt R W 'Bob' **4**, 6, 6, **7**, 8, 12–13, **13**, 15, **17**, 17, 20, 21–22, 24, 25, **3**(49, 91), 87
Fuge, Flg Off D E 34

Galton, Sqn Ldr Stan 76–77, **77**, 94
Gannon, Flt Lt Kevin 29, 46, 59
Garvan, Flt Lt Denis E W **33**, 34, 35
Gentry, WO C W 64, 65
Gibbes, Wg Cdr R H M 'Bobby' **31**(56, 94), 77, **79**, 79
Gibbs, Sqn Ldr 'Bill' **7**, 7, **10**, 10, 14–15, **15**, **16**, 17, 19–20, **21**, 21, 26, **5**(50, 91)
Gilbert, Sgt George **74**
Glaser, Flt Lt Dave **81**, 81, 93–94
Glendinning, Flt Lt A **27**(55, 94)
Goldsmith, Flt Lt Adrian P 'Tim' 12, **14**, 14, 15, 24–25, **12**(51, 92)
Goold, Flg Off Wilf 36, 40, 47, **48**, 48
Gossland, Flt Lt **81**, 81

Hall, Flt Lt E Smith 'Teddy' 12, **14**, **19**, 19, 22, **4**(49, 91)
Hamblyn, Flg Off D H 48

Hinds, WO 24
Hole, Flg Off C E M B 48
Holland, Sqn Ldr Bob 27, 28, 29
Hughes, Flg Off Tony **17**
Hunter, Flt Lt L T 'Babe' **63**, 64, 94
Hyde, Plt Off A 58
Hyde, Sgt Bill/Willie **28**, 29

Imphal 40, 41, 42, 44, 48, 58, 60
Indian Air Force, No 8 Sqn 66–67
Ingram, Sqn Ldr M R Bruce **31**, 31, **18**(53, 93), 60
Irvine, Plt Off F **70**

James, Flt Lt 'Jimmie' 39
James, Sqn Ldr Ken E 7, 23, **36**(57, 95), **80**
Japanese Army: 31st and 33rd Divisions 42; 55th Division 36–37
Japanese Army Air Force sentais: 8th 40, 41; 12th 32; 33rd 29; 50th 29, 45, 47–48, 59, 67, 69, 70; 55th 70; 59th 16; 61st 16; 64th 32, 34–35, 44–45, 47, 64, 65, 67, 69, 70, 94; 75th 18; 81st 28, 29, 46, 68; 204th 43, 45, 59
Japanese Naval Air Force, Imperial: 10th Sentai, 70th Independent Chutai **4**, 6, 11, 16, 23; 202nd Kokutai 9–10, 23; 753rd Kokutai 9–10
Jeffrey, Gp Capt Peter 25, 26, 80, 81, 91
Jenkins, Flt Sgt J R 15–16, 23
Jones, Flt Lt Norman **31**, 44

Kennedy, Flt Sgt E 58
Kennedy, Flt Sgt Pete 36
Kerr, Sqn Ldr Grant **72**
King, Flg Off J C 'Argus' 86
Kohima 42, 47
Krohn, Flt Lt I R 'Bats' 39, 41, 44, 46

Lacey, Sqn Ldr J H 'Ginger' **28**(55, 94), 61, **65**, 65–66, 68–69, **69**, **70**, 72
Laughton, Flt Lt L S 64
Lee, Wg Cdr Pat 30, 34, 47, **59**, 59
Linnard, Sqn Ldr 360 **22**(54, 93), 81
Louis, Flt Lt Paul G **28**, 28–29, **34**, 35, **14**(52, 92)

McCormack, Sqn Ldr D W 47, 58, 62
Macdonald, Flg Off R E J 31
MacDonald, Sqn Ldr Ron 17, 24
McDowell, Plt Off V 11, 22
McKay, Flt Sgt J 58
MacLean, Flt Lt Dean H 11, 18, **25**, 25–26
Mahoney, Flt Sgt 'Pat' **4**, 8
Mandalay 68, 69
Mawer, Flg Off Granville **13**, 13, 17
Meakin, Flt Lt Frederick **81**, 81
Mitsubishi: A6M Zero-sen 'Zeke' 11, 15, 25; Ki-46 'Dinah' **4**, 24
Moore, Flg Off 'Arch' 75
Morse, Plt Off 15

Nakajima: Ki-43 'Oscar' **47**; Ki-43-II 45–46; Ki-44 'Tojo' 35–36
Newman, Flt Lt Barney 87
Norwood, Flt Lt R K C **7**, 8, 13

operations: Ha-Go 37; Oboe 84; Thursday 41

Parker, WO W B 65
Partridge, WO R E **69**, 69–70
Patterson, Flt Sgt R O J 31
Pearl, Sqn Ldr Alan 29–30, 38, 39, 41, **43**, 43–44, 45–46, 48
Pegge, Sqn Ldr Constantine O J **34**(57, 95), **71**, **72**, 72
Potter, Sqn Ldr Cyril 69, 70
Pretty, Flg Off Jack 77, **78**, 78, 87

Rathwell, Flg Off Don 38, **39**, 45, 46, 47, 67–68, **68**
Rawlinson, Sqn Ldr Alan C **7**(50, 91), **73**, 73, **74**, 74
Read, Sgt 8
Reid, Flt Lt Len S **25**(55, 94), **76**, 76, **77**, 77, 79
Richards, Sqn Ldr Jim 75, 93
Riggall, Wg Cdr Robert F **66**, 66
Royal Air Force: AFTU, Armada Road **20**(53, 93), **60**, 60–61; No 165 Wing 30, 64; No 166 Wing 30; No 170 Wing 47; No 221 and 224 Groups 66; No 293 Wing 44; No 902 Wing 64; No 907 Wing **66**
Royal Air Force squadrons
  No 17: 40, **65**, 65–66, 67–69, **68**, 70, 72
  No 54: **4**, 6, **7**, 8, **9**, 10, 12, 13, **14**, **15**, 16, 17–18, 19–22, 26, **3**(49, 91), **5**, **6**(50, 91), **22**(54, 93), 79–80, 81–82, **82**; scoreboard 21
  No 67: 40, **16**(52, 92–93), **30**(56, 94), **61**, 61, 62, 67, 68
  No 81: 29, 38–39, **39**, 40, **41**, 41–44, **44**, 45, 46, 48, **17**(53, 93), 58, 59
  No 136: **27**, 28, 30, 31, 32, **33**, 33, 34, 35, 39–40, 41, 43, 44, 45, 47, **10**(51, 92), **19**(53, 93), 61; scoreboard 37
  No 152: 29, 30–31, 40, 44, 45, 47, **18**(53, 93), **32**(56, 94–95), 58, **59**, 61, 62, 63, 64, 65, 66, 68, **69**, 69–70, **72**; pilots **31**
  No 155: 33, 44, **26**, **28**(55, 94), **35**(57, 95), 62, **63**, 63, 64–65, 69, 70–71, **71**
  No 273: 61, 62, 64, 66, 69

No 548: 80, 81–82
No 549: **24**(54, 93–94), 80, **81**, 81–83; pilots **80**
Royal Australian Air Force: CGS, Cressy **23**(54, 93), **83**, 83; No 1 Fighter ('Churchill') Wing **4**, 6, 7, **8**, 8, **9**, 11–26, **12**, **1**(49, 91), 79–80, 81, 82–83; No 2 OTU 25, **9**(51, 92), 83; No 73 Wing 73, 76; No 80 Fighter Wing **29**, **31**(56, 94), 77, 78, **79**, 79, 80
Royal Australian Air Force squadrons
  No 79: **7**(50, 91), **25**(55, 94), **73**, 73–77, **74**, **75**, **76**, **77**, 79, 84, **86**, 86, 87
  No 85: **36**(57, 95), 80
  No 452: 7, 8, **11**, 11, 12, 13–14, **14**, 16–17, **18**, 18, 23, 24, **2**(49, 91), **8**(50, 91–92), **12**(51, 92), **13**(52, 92), **21**(54, 93), 77–78, **78**, 79–80, 80, 84, **85**, 85, 87; scoreboard **22**
  No 457: 7, 8, 9, 11, 14, 15–16, 17, **18**, 20, 22, 23, **24**, **25**, 25–26, **27**(55, 94), 77, 78, 79–80, **84**, 84–85, 87, 87
Royal Auxiliary Air Force squadrons
  No 607 'County of Durham' 28, **29**, 30, 31, 34, 36, 39, 40, 45, 46–48, **33**, **34**(57, 95), 58, 59, 61, 69, **71**, **72**; pilots 75
  No 615 'County of Surrey' 27–29, 30, 31, 32, **34**, 35, 35, 36, 40, 44, 46, 47, **14**, **15**(52, 92), **58**, 58, 59, **60**, 62, 69
Rudling, Flg Off Johnny **32**, 32, 47

Scrimgeour, Flt Lt S G 84–85, **85**, **87**
Sharkey, WO 68–69
Simpson, Flt Lt Clyde **67**, 67
Smith, Flg Off Len A **31**, 31, 38, **32**(56, 94–95), 65, 66, **69**
Smithson, Flg Off John H 17, **25**, 25, **26**, 26, **8**(50, 91–92)
Sole, WO G 36
Spencer, Flt Sgt G **15**
Steege, Wg Cdr Gordon 74
Stevenson, Flt Lt Mac 16
Storey, Sqn Ldr W Jack **23**(54, 93), **83**, 83
Supermarine Spitfire 27
Supermarine Spitfire Mark VC **8**, **12**, 15, 28, **78**, 87; A58-104 **23**(54, 93), **83**; A58-200 **76**; A58-220 **13**(52, 92); A58-248 **36**(57, 95); A58-252 **25**(55, 94), **77**; A58-254 **12**(51, 92); BR536 **15**; BR537 **18**; BR538 **24**; BR539 **7**, 13, **4**(49, 91); BR544 **7**; BS164 **7**, **10**, **15**, **5**(50, 91); BS181 **4**; **6**; BS186 **14**, **4**(49, 91); BS219 **20**; BS231 **11**, **2**(49, 91); BS295 **9**, **1**(49, 91); BS305 **13**, **6**(50, 91); EF543 **26**; ES307 **75**; JG740 **7**(50, 91); JG747 **34**; JG807 **11**(51, 92), **75**; JG891 **74**; JK225 **25**, **8**(50, 91–92); LZ862 **9**(51, 92); LZ975 **29**; MA292 **35**, **15**(52, 92); MA383 **27**, **10**(51, 92); MH300 **34**, **14**(52, 92); slipper tanks **36**, **76**
Supermarine Spitfire Mk VIII 29–30, **39**, 39, **41**, 44, 45–46, 63; A58-354 **22**(54, 93); A58-379 **24**(54, 93–94), **81**; A58-435 **21**(54, 93); **80**; A58-480 **82**; A58-514 **27**(55, 94); A58-528 **29**(56, 94), **78**; A58-602 **31**(56, 94), **79**; A58-605 **86**; A58-620 **84**; A58-631 **87**; JF698 **41**, **17**(53, 93); JF835 **18**(53, 93); JF902 **66**; JG183 **66**; JG534 **33**(57, 95); JG560 **20**(53, 93), **60**; JG567 **30**(56, 94); JG606 **60**; JG614 **65**; JG813 **16**(52, 92–93); LV678 **26**(55, 94), **63**, 63; MD215 **28**(55, 94); MD373 **58**; MT567 **19**(53, 93); MT791 **71**; MT879 **32**(56, 94–95); MT904 **34**(57, 95), **71**; MT982 **72**; MV406 **69**; MV483 **35**(57, 95), **71**; 'YB-M' **68**
Supermarine Spitfire Mk XIV 72

Taylor, Flg Off Horace 46–47, 59
Thompson, Flt Lt R S 70
Thorold-Smith, Sqn Ldr Raymond E 'Throttle' 7, **11**, 11, 13, **2**(49, 91)

Unstead, Flt Sgt E 68

Vanderfield, Flt Lt R Doug **11**(51, 92), **73**, 73, **75**
Varney, Flt Sgt Frank 8, 12
Vickers, WO J W 58, 65, 68
Vincent, AVM Stanley 42

Waddy, Flt Lt John L 25, **9**(51, 92), 83
Walker, Gp Capt B R 82
Wall, Flg Off 14
Walters, Gp Capt Alan 'Wally' 8, 18
Watson, Sqn Ldr Bruce 8
Watson, Flt Lt Philip 12, 15, 16, 22, 23
Watson, WO C M G 62
Watson, Flt Sgt Rex 12, 15, **20**, 22, **23**, 23
Watts, Sqn Ldr R A 82
Weggery, Flt Lt S Lawrence E **28**, 28–29, **35**, 35, 47, **15**(52, 92)
Wettenhall, Flt Lt Llewellyn 75
Wheeler, Sgt David 17–18
Whitamore, Sqn Ldr W M 'Babe' 38, 42, 43, 44, **17**(53, 93)
White, Lt J G 46, 58
Wilding, Flg Off Frank E **33**, 40
Wilkinson, Wg Cdr Roy 82
Witteridge, Flg Off Albert H 'Witt' **26**(55, 94), **63**, 63, 64, 65
Wright, Sgt D L 32

Yates, Plt Off 'Banger' **34**, 36, **40**, 40
Young, Flt Sgt H K **27**, 58, 92